TO KNOW THIS LOVE

OTHER BOOKS BY DAN WILT

Jesus in the Wild: Lessons on Calling for Life in the World by Dan Wilt

Receive the Holy Spirit: A 70-Day Journey through the Scriptures by Dan Wilt

Roots: Advent and the Family Story of Jesus by Dan Wilt

MORE DAILY READERS FROM SEEDBED

The Advent Mission: Advent by Omar Rikabi

Between You and Me: 2 John, 3 John, Philemon, Titus, and Jude by Omar Rikabi

Behold, the Man: John by J. D. Walt

The Christian New Year: Advent by J. D. Walt

The Domino Effect: Colossians by J. D. Walt

First Love: Philippians by J. D. Walt

The First Real Christian: James by J. D. Walt

First Word. Last Word. God's Word: The Bible by J. D. Walt

First Word. Last Word. God's Word: Volume Two by J. D. Walt

The Gospel of the Holy Spirit: Mark by J. D. Walt

Listen to Him: Lent by J. D. Walt

People Who Say Such Things: Faith by J. D. Walt

Protagonist: Advent by Matt LeRoy and Josh LeRoy

Right Here, Right Now, Jesus: Prayer by J. D. Walt

This Is How We Know: 1 John by J. D. Walt

(un)Puzzled: Ephesians by J. D. Walt

What Happens in Corinth: 1 Corinthians by J. D. Walt

Wilderness: Exodus by J. D. Walt

TO KNOW THIS LOVE

Discovering Our Union with God in Christ

DAN WILT

Page design and layout by PerfecType, Nashville, Tennessee

Wilt, Dan.
  To know this love / Dan Wilt. – Franklin, Tennessee : Seedbed Publishing, ©2024.

  pages ; cm.

  ISBN: 9798888000878 (paperback)
  ISBN: 9798888000885 (epub)
  ISBN: 9798888000892 (pdf)
  OCLC: 1478024279

  1. God--Love--Biblical teaching. 2. Bible--Love--Meditations.
  3. Mystical union--Biblical teaching. 4. Mystical union--Meditations.
  5. Bible. Ephesians, III, 14-21--Meditations. I. Title.

BS680.L64.W54 2024   252./62   2024952525

SEEDBED PUBLISHING
Franklin, Tennessee
seedbed.com

CONTENTS

INTRODUCTION

Several years ago I set out to write about the topic of love in the Scriptures. With my laptop powered on and the Scriptures open before me, I was ready to begin. My goal was simple: I wanted to clarify what love truly meant when it was spoken by Jesus or his followers—both for myself and for others. I especially wanted to write about love for my children, and for their ongoing awareness of the love Jesus has for each of them.

The writing was to be an extended pastoral meditation on the topic of love in the Bible, given the many (and often impoverished) meanings assigned to the word in our day. Social media is rife with versions of love that, at their best, leave people wanting, and, at their worst, damage the heart.

I vividly remember sitting at my desk that day, my heart full with an overwhelming awareness of just how beloved I was to God. I also felt, deep in my bones, just how beloved everyone I knew—and did not know—was to God.

Just as I began writing, simultaneously praying for humility and revelation, I had a pause in my heart. I had a realization that was beginning to flourish into a revelation, and it halted me.

I had opened books, recalled stories, gathered quotes, and took long swims in the deep waters of the Bible—particularly the Gospels and the New Testament. And as I did, I continually came upon *another* theme that seemed to be inseparable from the vision of love taught by Jesus, and then by Paul.

Just as one frequency resonates with another when played on an instrument, this emerging theme resonated every time the idea of love was played.

And what was that theme? It was the theme of *union with God in Christ.*

UNION WITH CHRIST AND FULLNESS OF LOVE

There is no Christian I know, at least among those who are serious about their faith, who does not want to be *one* with Christ.

We want to abide in him, as he abides in us (John 15:4–5; 17:23). We want to be "united with him" in his death and resurrection (Rom. 6:5–11). We want to be one with him in Spirit (1 Cor. 6:17). We know the language, and our hearts are attuned to knowing Jesus in the very best way we can this side of heaven.

But what do these verses mean in our day-to-day living?

As I began to explore the theme of union with God, what it means to participate, person-to-Person, in the very life of God, I saw that the two streams of love and union were actually forming one great and mighty river.

Union with God in Christ was not a *side-theme* of love—the two themes were *one*. One cannot experience the fullness of love without experiencing union with Jesus. One cannot experience the fullness of union with Jesus without experiencing love.

Jesus's teaching in John 14, 15, and 17, and Paul's writing as he engaged phrases like "in Christ" and "in Christ Jesus" all had a part to play in this revelation. I began to see Paul's writing on being "in Christ" and his writing on the love of God in a new, blended light.

As I read Paul's writing, I began to ask a question I had not previously asked myself: "How did a zealous, murderous Pharisee become regarded as one of the world's greatest poets on love (i.e., 1 Corinthians 13)?"

What, or rather, *Who*, happened to him?

Acts 9, the story of Paul's conversion, began to lift off the page. I started to see that familiar and almost journalistic story brimming with, of all things, *love*. Could it be that at the center of Paul's encounter on the road to Damascus was a profound experience with the *love* of Jesus—divine love forming the core of his powerful encounter with the one he was persecuting?

And could it be that's Paul's conversion by love is what precipitated the overwhelming and pervasive theme of love in what we know as the Pauline letters? I could not unsee what I was seeing. Paul wrote about many things, including faith, hope, and love. But for him, the "greatest of these is *love*" (1 Cor. 13:13, emphasis mine).

TO KNOW THIS LOVE

As I meditated on Paul's letters, I felt him searching, as I or any writer would, for ample words to describe the indescribable, his sense of participation in the very life of Jesus.

Consider how Paul so poetically pens his prayer in Ephesians 3:

> And I pray that you, being rooted and established in love, may have power, together with all the Lord's holy people, to grasp how wide and long and high and deep is the love of Christ, and *to know this love* that surpasses knowledge—that you may be filled to the measure of all the fullness of God. (vv. 17b–19, emphasis mine)

To know this love. That was Paul's goal for his own life, and for ours. He wanted us to know this love that transcends, and gives meaning to, all other loves. Then, he wanted Jesus to live his life of love through him (Gal. 2:20), and to become like Jesus to others in all respects.

As I began to write, the ideas of union with Christ and love became inseparable. Experiencing the love of

God and extending the reach of that divine love into the world has everything to do with living—in a very real, practical, and personal sense—in *union* with Christ. I would say it this way, to summarize the central thesis of this book: *The goal of the Christian life is union with God in Christ.*

A JOURNEY TOGETHER

In the following pages we will take a fifty-day journey together exploring the biblical, theological idea of *union with God in Christ.* We will explore its connection to both receiving God's love and then becoming the love of God to the world.

It is union with God in Christ that enables us to die with Jesus, to be raised to life with him (Rom. 6:4–8), and to live in him over a lifetime. We can participate in the divine nature of Jesus because of union (1 Peter 1:3–4). And that union makes us people who are receptive to God's transcendent love, and capable of offering it—sacrificially and as people who live cruciform (cross-shaped) lives—to the world God loves (John 3:16).

This book is a long reflection on these ideas to serve your daily walk with Jesus. These readings are not intended to form a theological work (though they are full of theology). Neither are they intended to cover all the passages nor ideas associated with union and love in the Bible.

Rather, they are intended to be pastoral and encouraging to you in your union with Jesus, as you live into it each and every day. I hope this book will serve you in your ongoing sense of communion with, participation in, and presence to our Lord Jesus.

And I pray your awareness of the love Jesus has for you, and your love for Jesus, would deepen and increase as you read and pray through these pages.

I look forward to a special, life-changing journey ahead. I know that my life has been changed by writing *To Know This Love*—may you be able to say the same by the time you finish this book.

May we all come into the unity of the faith (Eph. 4:13) that is found only in union with Jesus. May his love abound to you, in you, more and more in knowledge and depth of insight (Phil. 1:9–11), and may he bind your heart in union to his as he intends.

In Christ Jesus, with you,

Dan Wilt
Franklin, Tennessee

1

INTO UNION AND LOVE

JOHN 15:4–5

"Remain in me, as I also remain in you. No branch can bear fruit by itself; it must remain in the vine. Neither can you bear fruit unless you remain in me. I am the vine; you are the branches. If you remain in me and I in you, you will bear much fruit; apart from me you can do nothing."

CONSIDER THIS

The parking garage was almost full, so I had to park on the very top level. Deciding to walk down the steps instead of taking the elevator (a good health choice, I told myself), I entered the open stairwell. As I approached the first landing, I heard a strange, rustling sound below me on the next level down. It sounded like the fluttering of wings. But then, after each fluttering sound, I heard erratic thudding noises, as if something was bumping against a wall.

With some degree of trepidation, I slowly made my way down the steps, trying to guess what sight was about to greet me. To my astonishment, there on a ledge stood a mourning dove—trembling and appearing distressed. Its neck was frayed thin and its feathers lay strewn on the steps. In front of the dove, bolted tight to the ledge on which it stood, was a thick sheet of plexiglass, presumably installed on the stairwell to keep birds from flying into the parking garage. I then realized what was happening. This poor dove was trapped *inside* by the barrier intended to keep it *outside*. Through the glass, the bewildered bird could see the green trees for which it longed, its home and probable nesting place. This beautiful, dappled creature had been struggling, perhaps for hours or more, to get past the invisible membrane keeping it from its destiny.

Startled by my presence, the small creature thrust itself into the air once again in a renewed attempt to fly to the trees. *Thud.* I watched the dove fall awkwardly to the ledge, stunned and exhausted. The bird could see the *goal* but could not reach it in its own strength.

And here we see a metaphor for life as a follower of Jesus. The dove's predicament mirrored that of a Christian who can see, even taste, the fullness of life in Christ for which they long. They know all the passages about dwelling *in* Christ, *in* his love, but they just can't seem to get there from here. Faith-frazzled and spiritually

DAN WILT

spent, many of us will bang our head against the glass of our daily longing for a lifetime, seeing the goal before us yet never being able to touch it. We may even build a theology around that struggle, believing it is the lot of the Christian to live a form of futile spiritual existence, a kind of carrot-in-front-of-the-donkey faith, as the dream of the abundant life Jesus promised eludes us.

Many followers of Jesus I know, including myself at times, have found themselves harried and near death as we engage our best efforts to follow Jesus. When those best efforts fail us, we may not lose our faith, but we may certainly diminish in our hope. Our dreams of spiritual fulfillment, of closeness with Jesus, of experiencing his love for us, of loving others from the overflow of a full heart, become very, very small. We may know, intellectually, that we are loved by God. We may even know that we are designed to carry that divine love into the world around us. But still we remain disheveled and broken on the ledge, seeing what we believe to be our inheritance in Jesus before us but bereft of the means to access it.

According to Jesus and the promises of Scripture, today your story and mine can *change*. What if Jesus gave us the key to experiencing fullness of life and love in him, marked by a deepening awareness of our belovedness and a consistent ability to embody that love to the world God loves? And what if we have simply misunderstood how life *in Christ*, in Jesus, actually works? What if our best efforts fail us by design, in order that we might descend to new depths of humility and surrender in our union with Jesus—and that is the way forward?

Let's return to our story of the mourning dove. I moved slowly, resting my open hand on the ledge, and began to speak gently—even lovingly—to the bird. As I edged closer, it was as if God spoke to the dove. Quivering, and drained from its desperate quest for freedom, it tentatively waddled close to me—and literally collapsed into my waiting hand. I slowly lifted my other hand to envelope the bird, tucking the tired creature close to my chest. Then I instinctively turned us both away from the glass and the trees. I looked into the dove's tiny eyes and whispered, "I've got you. You can trust me." (I like to believe animals understand tone and sound even if they can't understand language.) I descended with the bird to the next level down (another metaphor, of course), seeing there was no glass below. Then, gently thrusting my hands forward over the railing, I released the small pilgrim into the air. The dove stretched its fragile wings and shot through the air, straight for the trees—disappearing from sight.

As it is for us, the dove's freedom was on the other side of its greatest struggle. It was on the other side of complete surrender. It was on the other side of descent. Most importantly, the bird's freedom was on the other side of connection and closeness with me—the only one who had the compassion, power, and knowledge to take it where it wanted to go.

Jesus invited us to abide, to remain, to dwell in him. He told us that he himself would abide, remain, and dwell in us. What if this invitation was more than an encouragement, more than a series of pleasant metaphorical, relational words? What if our lives will be an endless banging against spiritual glass until we turn the gaze of our heart completely—without reserve—toward Jesus? And what if we can only do that because the Spirit of Jesus himself is *actually dwelling in us*, empowering us to do so from within, making the abundant life we seek possible? What if living in complete, real communion with Jesus—hearing his voice, knowing his will, experiencing his love, and naturally sharing that love with others—is only attainable through a realized, Holy Spirit *union* with Jesus?

Today, you are invited to share in the very life of God—the Father, the Son, and the Holy Spirit. If you are ready to say yes to that invitation, let's begin.

THE PRAYER

Lord Jesus, I am in you and you are in me. Like that mourning dove, I realize that it is only in union with you, experienced in my complete surrender to your love and purposes, that I can enjoy the abundant life you have promised. I fall into your hands today. Live your life, by your Spirit, through me. I want to be one with you; this is my highest goal. In Christ Jesus, I pray, amen.

THE QUESTIONS

- Have you ever felt like that dove, trapped behind glass and feeling like you are getting nowhere in your walk with Jesus?

- Have you experienced a time when you felt you had come to the very end of your efforts to experience God's love or to share it with others, only to find that the way forward was through surrender, allowing God to draw you close in your time of greatest weakness?

2

THE PRAYER OF UNION AND LOVE

EPHESIANS 3:14–21

For this reason I kneel before the Father, from whom every family in heaven and on earth derives its name. **I pray that out of his glorious riches he may strengthen you with power through his Spirit in your inner being**, so that Christ may dwell in your hearts through faith. And I pray that you, being rooted and established in love, may have power, together with all the Lord's holy people, to grasp how wide and long and high and deep is the love of Christ, and to know this love that surpasses knowledge—that you may be filled to the measure of all the fullness of God.

Now to him who is able to do immeasurably more than all we ask or imagine, according to his power that is at work within us, to him be glory in the church and in Christ Jesus throughout all generations, for ever and ever! Amen.

CONSIDER THIS

Who do you want to become? What kind of person do you hope to be?

Here is my answer to those two questions: I want to be transformed into someone who lives, day after day and year after year, in complete union with Jesus. I want to be the kind of person who is filled to overflowing with his love, who is one with him in my thoughts, feelings, and actions, and who is surrendered to his Spirit living through me—touching the lives of everyone I meet. Is that your desire as well? If so, today's journey to becoming that kind of a person can begin with a *prayer*.

The prayer of Ephesians 3:14–21 is eight verses long. It was written by the apostle Paul from prison to brothers and sisters in Ephesus whom he cared deeply about. The prayer is full of *intercession* (he is praying for us), *faith* (he clearly believes what he's praying), and *love* (his love overflows into the goal that we as readers experience the love God has for us). The prayer is directed to God the Father and is one of the most beautiful, profound, worshipful, and love-centered prayers of the New Testament.

What may not be so obvious is that the majority of what Paul is praying in this passage is deeply rooted in the teaching of Jesus (more on that later). I like to call this prayer our entry point, the Prayer of Union and Love. Let's go a little deeper.

Paul is *interceding*. He is asking for something of the Father, with *faith*, for the rest of us. As he prays, it would seem as though he is overcome by *love*—love for God and

     DAN WILT

for his people. Read the passage out loud, with enthusiasm, and you'll see what I mean. From what seems to be a wellspring of worship bursting from his heart, Paul pours out his request for the saints in Ephesus—and for you and me today.

As I read the prayer, he seems to be praying for two things:

- That we would have power to *experience union* with the indwelling Jesus (vv. 16–17), and
- That we would have power to *know the fullness of Christ's love* for us (vv. 17–19).

I actually believe that Paul is praying for us that we would reach the goal of the Christian life: *union with God in Christ.* And that union, in both the Gospels and Paul's letters, is often spoken of in the context of Christ's love.

Paul wants us to be one with Jesus, who lives in us, and to know the fullness of his love for us. That is where the whole salvation project in your life and mine is headed. Not just forgiveness for sin. Not mere acceptance or tolerance on God's part. Not more religious activities stacked on your already congested schedule. Certainly not a ticket to heaven.

Union with God in Christ—that is the hope toward which we are all headed.

Now let's take Paul's prayer for us one step further. Let's try personalizing it, for ourselves (I) and for our community (we), with some small adaptations. This is a practice called "praying Scripture," making a passage into a prayer that resonates with the abiding truths of God's Word:

> *I/we kneel before you, Father, from whom every family in heaven and on earth derives its name. I/ we pray that out of your glorious riches you would strengthen me/us with power through your Spirit in my/our inner being, so that Christ may dwell in my/our heart(s) through faith. And I pray that I/ we, being rooted and established in love, may have power, together with all the Lord's holy people, to grasp how wide and long and high and deep is the love of Christ, and to know this love that surpasses knowledge—that I/we may be filled to the measure of all the fullness of God. Now to you who are able to do immeasurably more than all I/we ask or imagine, according to your power that is at work within me/ us, to you be glory in the church and in Christ Jesus throughout all generations, for ever and ever! Amen.*

This Prayer of Union and Love will become our prayer for this journey together. Paul knew we would need God's power to apprehend what it means to have Jesus living in us. He also knew that we would need power to comprehend the expansive love Christ has for us. Human attempts to understand an indwelling

God will fail us. Human efforts to conjure up a sense of Christ's love toward us will leave us empty. With this prayer, we are praying for God to do what only God can do: to reveal the reality of his abiding in us, and the incomparable nature of the love that pursues you and me each day.

We'll take the next few days to explore the riches in this prayer.

THE PRAYER

Lord Jesus, I am in you and you are in me. I pray that true spiritual longing would be stirred in my heart today—longing to experience a fullness of relationship with you and longing to experience the fullness of your love. I want to live in union with you as you live in me, "filled to the measure of all the fullness of God." In Christ Jesus, I pray, amen.

THE QUESTIONS

- Have you ever had an experience when you felt like you were one with God? What was your experience like, and how did it change you?

3

UNION WITH CHRIST

EPHESIANS 3:14–21

For this reason I kneel before the Father, from whom every family in heaven and on earth derives its name. I pray that out of his glorious riches he may strengthen you with power through his Spirit in your inner being, so **that Christ may dwell in your hearts through faith.** And I pray that you, being rooted and established in love, may have power, together with all the Lord's holy people, to grasp how wide and long and high and deep is the love of Christ, and to know this love that surpasses knowledge—that you may be filled to the measure of all the fullness of God.

Now to him who is able to do immeasurably more than all we ask or imagine, according to his power that is at work within us, to him be glory in the church and in Christ Jesus throughout all generations, for ever and ever! Amen.

CONSIDER THIS

When our young family moved into our first home, we were ecstatic. It was very small, but as the old saying goes, it was a palace to us. I remember my wife and I standing in our tiny living room, realizing what had just happened: We bought a house! We were the king and queen of our very own little castle!

Ready to move in, we had boxes waiting outside and our friends gathered to help. We felt so thankful—and we were eager to get settled in.

We were about to *inhabit* the house.

Nothing about that house would ever be the same once we made it our dwelling place. My wife's sense of decor would transform the barest room into a sanctuary of rest and peace. Pictures would cover the walls, reminders of our family members and what was truly important to us. Once we were fully moved in, the house became like an extension of us. The rooms were expressions of our life together. That address marked the spot where our days, nights, love, learning, and joy were shared.

In the first part of Paul's prayer, in verse 17, he prays: "I pray that out of his glorious riches he may strengthen you with power through his Spirit in your inner being, so that *Christ may dwell in your hearts through faith*." What does this part of the prayer mean?

New Testament scholar Ben Witherington writes this: "Paul is praying for the continuing presence of Christ within the Christians through faith. The verb *katoikeō* signifies literally to make a home or to settle down and so has in view a more permanent presence."[1]

With this insight in mind, the verse means that Jesus has moved in—and it takes the eyes of faith ("Faith is confidence in what we hope for and assurance about what we do not see" [Heb. 11:1]) to continually see it. This is a prayer for an intimate awareness that Jesus is *abiding* in us by the Holy Spirit; inhabiting our hearts in a way that is as real and as true as my family inhabiting that house.

Paul is harkening back to the teaching of Jesus in John 14 and 15, where Jesus speaks boldly about the human heart becoming the place in which the Father and the Son will make their home (14:23). The Spirit will live within us as in a temple (John 14:17; 1 Cor. 6:19). Jesus will be in us, the Father will be in Jesus, and Jesus will be in the Father (John 14:10–11, 16–17, 20).

Jesus has moved into the house of your heart and made it his home. It takes faith to believe this and to live from this unseen reality. But the more our faith grows, the more experience we have with Christ living his life through us (Gal. 2:20), and the more we see what is actually happening. Jesus has made his home in us. He is inhabiting our hearts. Our life belongs to him, and his

---

1. Ben Witherington, *The Letters to Philemon, the Colossians, and the Ephesians: A Socio-Rhetorical Commentary on the Captivity Epistles* (Grand Rapids: Wm. B. Eerdmans Publishing, 2007), 274.

     DAN WILT

transformation of the place is being seen everywhere (1 Cor. 6:19–20). You might say that Jesus gets to rearrange the furniture.

A short form way to say that Christ is living within us, inhabiting us, is the word *union*. We are living in *union* with Christ. This a word we'll use time and time again to refer to us living in Jesus, and Jesus living in us. And from that union, God is reshaping our personality, our desires, and our lives to conform to the likeness of his Son (Rom. 8:29; 2 Cor. 3:18).

What if we allowed Jesus to do a true conversion of our heart, mind, and even body? What if we believed that it is true when Paul says that the mystery of the gospel is "Christ in you" (Col. 1:27)? What if we awakened, arose from our spiritual slumber, by the words, "Do you not realize that Christ Jesus is in you?" (2 Cor. 13:5), and began to live as the habitation of Jesus?

You and I were made to abide in Christ, and to have Christ abide in us (John 15:4–5). This is where the adventure begins.

THE PRAYER

Lord Jesus, I am in you and you are in me. I want to become, more and more every day, the place of your habitation. Change me as you will, as I learn what it means to live in union with you. In Christ Jesus, I pray, amen.

THE QUESTIONS

- What other metaphors come to mind when you think about Jesus living in you, and you living in Jesus?

- Pause now and ask the question: How has my life changed since Jesus moved in?

4

ROOTED AND ESTABLISHED IN LOVE

EPHESIANS 3:14–21

For this reason I kneel before the Father, from whom every family in heaven and on earth derives its name. I pray that out of his glorious riches he may strengthen you with power through his Spirit in your inner being, so that Christ may dwell in your hearts through faith. And I pray that you, **being rooted and established in love**, may have power, together with all the Lord's holy people, to grasp how wide and long and high and deep is the love of Christ, and to know this love that surpasses knowledge—that you may be filled to the measure of all the fullness of God.

Now to him who is able to do immeasurably more than all we ask or imagine, according to his power that is at work within us, to him be glory in the church and in Christ Jesus throughout all generations, for ever and ever! Amen.

Hydrangeas are fascinating plants.

Not only are they beautiful, but they can change according to their conditions. My wife has taught me that if we change the acidity of the soil in which hydrangeas are growing—the ones outside our kitchen window that elicit oohs and aahs from all who visit each year—we can actually change the color of the blooms themselves. If I sprinkle enough coffee grounds on the soil throughout the year, the hydrangea petals will change from pink to purple, to a vivid blue. Honestly, it's like an explosion of color right outside our window each May!

For the hydrangea, the soil can *change* the flower. That's not all the soil does, as we know. The soil is what gives the plant sustenance and life. If the soil is right, the plant will thrive. If the soil is wrong, the plant will wither. And this is especially true: if the plant is not firmly rooted and established in the soil that gives it life, the plant will surely die.

In Ephesians 3:14–21, Paul wants his family in Christ to be "rooted and established" in the nutritious soil of the love of God. N. T. Wright says this of the prayer:

Essentially, it is a prayer that the young Christians may discover the heart of what it means to be a Christian. It means knowing God as the all-loving, all-powerful father; it means putting down roots into that love. . . . It means having that love turn into a well-directed and effective energy in one's personal life. And it means the deep and powerful knowing and loving into which the Christian is invited to enter; or—to put the same thing another way—the knowing and loving which should enter into the Christian. Paul, quite clearly, knows this in his own experience. He longs that those who have come to put their **faith** in Jesus should know it too.[2]

Ben Witherington adds: "One can grasp it [Christ's love] only through experience, and even when one experiences it one is left groping for words to describe it. The ultimate goal of being rooted in love and grasping its meaning is to 'be filled in all the fullness of God.'"[3]

Like the soil of those hydrangeas, the type of love in which we are rooted has everything to do with the type of person we are becoming. There are many different kinds of lesser-love soils out there diminishing the color and health of people's lives.

Putting our roots deep into the love of the Father for us—resulting in a person-to-Person union (knowing)

---

2. N. T. Wright, *Paul for Everyone: The Prison Letters* (Louisville: Westminster John Knox Press, 2004), 39–40, emphasis original.

3. Ben Witherington, *The Letters to Philemon, the Colossians, and the Ephesians: A Socio-Rhetorical Commentary on the Captivity Epistles* (Grand Rapids: Wm. B. Eerdmans Publishing, 2007), 275.

and intimacy (loving)—is the way to being "filled to the measure of all the fullness of God."

THE PRAYER

Lord Jesus, I am in you and you are in me. Like a plant growing in your garden, bearing the kinds of blossoms and fragrance (2 Cor. 2:15) that rise from the soil in which I am rooted, I want to be rooted firmly in your love. Take me deeper into union with you, so the flowers of my life express your heart and character in the world. In Christ Jesus, I pray, amen.

THE QUESTIONS

- If you were to check the health of the soil in which you have planted your life, how would you describe its quality? Is it the healthy soil of the Father's kind and healing love for you? Or is it a mix of that soil with some other soils—lesser-love soils that may actually be hindering your growth?

- What soil do you want to be rooted and established in today, and why?

5

EXPERIENCING LOVE

EPHESIANS 3:14–21

For this reason I kneel before the Father, from whom every family in heaven and on earth derives its name. I pray that out of his glorious riches he may strengthen you with power through his Spirit in your inner being, so that Christ may dwell in your hearts through faith. And I pray that you, being rooted and established in love, may have power, together with all the Lord's holy people, **to grasp how wide and long and high and deep is the love of Christ, and to know this love that surpasses knowledge**—that you may be filled to the measure of all the fullness of God.

Now to him who is able to do immeasurably more than all we ask or imagine, according to his power that is at work within us, to him be glory in the church and in Christ Jesus throughout all generations, for ever and ever! Amen.

CONSIDER THIS

Today, I'd like to begin with a personal story as we consider verses 18–19 of the Prayer of Union and Love in Ephesians 3:14–21.

Jesus drew me to himself in my high school years. I made a profession of faith, and I was touched deeply by the grace and love of God. But in my first year of university, I had a new, profound encounter with the love of God—one that has forever changed me.

I was home on break from university. I was sitting on my bed, in the upstairs bedroom of my childhood home. I was struggling with the intellectual challenges to my growing faith that I was experiencing at Penn State University. Those challenges orbited around the readings and class discussions in my religion course. My professor was a former pastor and an avowed agnostic. I was in a state of spiritual distress—not caused particularly by him or by my classmates—but by my incessant mulling over the ideas we were exploring. It made my sleep restless, and I was preoccupied with my questions when awake.

I could not have put words to it then, but I was experiencing spiritual longing, an inner yearning that accompanied my inward turmoil. It was a longing for a new way of knowing God, a fullness of experience of his person, that was stronger than any I had ever known. It was like I was living out the words of Psalm 42:2—"My soul thirsts for God, for the living God. When can I go and meet with God?" I know now that I was seeking a personal awakening.

As I sat on my bed, praying through my fragmented emotions, something happened. I can't express the entire experience, but I will describe the best part of it. Imagine a swollen river of Jesus's love for me, held back by a thick dam. Now imagine that dam bursting. My questions, my doubts, my cynicism, my fears—all were swept up in the river of the Spirit rushing through me. Love was unleashed full force on my soul. I was having my own personal upper-room experience!

I was undone; I wept and sobbed for joy on my bed. I found my hands raised in the air, my body shaking, and my mind clear of its previous confusion. In what seemed to be an instant, I felt seen and known to my very core; I was caught up in a state I can only describe as bliss. I felt at one with God . . . filled with him, and loved to my core.

After that experience, I didn't feel as though I knew Jesus rationally like one would know the answer to a math equation. I felt as though I knew Jesus relationally like one would know someone you dearly love has just entered the room. This was a heart-knowing, a person encountering a Person—and something deep in my heart was settled.

In the beautiful book *Sola Sancta Caritas*, Joe Dongell writes these words about John Wesley's understanding of the importance of experiencing the love God has for us:

> If love is a gift from God, then we must seek to receive love from God, the very love we are commanded to then express both to God and to others. . . . The mere fact that one is a Christian,

even a spiritually gifted and effective person, is not yet proof that one has undergone the deeper reception of God's love. Love is something we must, apparently, seek (just as Paul urges in 1 Cor. 14:1), and must seek with the expectation that God will (in his own time and way) actually satisfy this quest.[4]

I like to think that Wesley's experiences were similar to my own, perhaps his most well-known being his Aldersgate experience on May 24, 1738. This is when he famously said his heart was "strangely warmed." But at Fetter Lane on January 1, 1739, as he gathered with others for prayer on New Year's, we sense a tone that is somewhat different in character, if not intensity, from what happened at Aldersgate:

> Mr. Hall, Kinchin, Ingham, [George] Whitefield, Hutchins, and my brother Charles were present at our love feast in Fetter Lane, with about sixty of our brethren. About three in the morning, as we were continuing instant in prayer, the power of God came mightily upon us, insomuch that many cried out for exceeding joy, and many fell to the ground. As soon as we recovered a little from that awe and amazement at the presence

---

4. Joseph Dongell, *Sola Sancta Caritas* (Franklin, TN: Seedbed Publishing, 2006), 32.

  DAN WILT

of his majesty, we broke out with one voice, "We praise thee, O God; we acknowledge thee to be the Lord."[5]

Your experiences of God's love may be very different from mine or Wesley's. I certainly have not had another one like the experience I described since. But I somehow imagine that Paul would have smiled, and understood all the kinds of experiences with the love of God noted by saints throughout history, and experienced by you and me on a day-to-day basis. Paul's own conversion, which we will explore soon, may have had some of the same characteristics.

I am grateful that Jesus reaches into our lives, meets us in our spiritual confusion and religious ruts, and surpasses our knowledge with his love. He is truly the lover of our souls.

THE PRAYER

Lord Jesus, I am in you and you are in me. I want to experience all that you have for me in this life. I receive your presence in me, and your love for me, by faith. I also welcome you to interrupt my life with encounters with you that take me deeper into the reality of your love for me and our union. In Christ Jesus, I pray, amen.

---

5. John Telford, *The Life of John Wesley* (London: The Epworth Press, 1947), 394.

- Can you relate an experience you have had on your journey with Jesus to one of the experiences shared? What happened, and how have you been changed by it?

     DAN WILT

6

ALL THE FULLNESS OF GOD

EPHESIANS 3:14–21

For this reason I kneel before the Father, from whom every family in heaven and on earth derives its name. I pray that out of his glorious riches he may strengthen you with power through his Spirit in your inner being, so that Christ may dwell in your hearts through faith. And I pray that you, being rooted and established in love, may have power, together with all the Lord's holy people, to grasp how wide and long and high and deep is the love of Christ, and to know this love that surpasses knowledge—**that you may be filled to the measure of all the fullness of God.**

Now to him who is able to do immeasurably more than all we ask or imagine, according to his power that is at work within us, to him be glory in the church and in Christ Jesus throughout all generations, for ever and ever! Amen.

CONSIDER THIS

When you think about being "filled" with God's Spirit, what metaphors come to mind? If you are like me, one visual image usually leads the way—a vessel being filled to the brim with God's presence. But there are other ways we can think about spiritual fullness, ways that may help us better understand what Paul is getting at when he writes, "that you may be filled to the measure of all the fullness of God." Here are just a few.

When the night sky is radiant with light, we say it is *full* of stars. When we are moved by affection for someone we care about, we say that we are *full* of love for that person. When orchestral music is strong and encompassing, we say the music sounds *full* and strong. When a season of time is complete, we may say that season has reached a *full*ness of time (Gal. 4:4). When a young person becomes an adult, we say that they have come to *full* maturity.

With these ideas in mind, as we read verse 19, spiritual fullness can mean a number of things: we are radiant with Christ, permeated with Christ, encompassed and moved by Christ, complete in Christ, and mature in Christ. It can also mean we are overflowing with Christ.

Then, zooming out a bit more on Ephesians 3:14–21, we see that the goal of spiritual fullness is actually the point of Paul's prayer.

Verses 16–17 point to verse 19: "I pray . . . that Christ may dwell in your hearts through faith" (vv. 16–17) "*. . . that you may be filled to the measure of all the fullness of God*" (v. 19, emphasis mine).

 DAN WILT

Verses 17–18 also point to verse 19: "I pray that you . . . may have power . . . to grasp" (vv. 17–18) "and to know this love . . . *that you may be filled to the measure of all the fullness of God*" (v. 19, emphasis mine).

Paul clearly wants us to be filled with God and his love. And what is his measure? "Filled to the measure of all the fullness of God" means that God's person is the quantitative standard, the measure. But God is boundless and endless. So, to put it another way, the God-measure is the measure beyond all measures, the metric beyond all metrics! Paul is praying that we are to be filled with God, beyond ourselves, beyond understanding, beyond-all-limits—*full* in a God-sized way!

Our Creator is not primarily interested in us coming into the fullness of who *we* are, at least not as the end goal. Our Creator is interested in us coming into the fullness of who *he* is—in character, love, and wholeness. Made in the image of God, the *imago Dei*, we are unique personalities reflecting God's glory into the world. Our Father intends for us to thrive and delight in our uniqueness—but not to see self-expression as the culmination of our destiny.

Our identity as image-bearers is to be filled and radiant with Christ's presence. Just as a unique and remarkable stained glass window shines with light from within, so, too, we remain uniquely beautiful as the light of Jesus shines through our gifts and personalities.

Our Father wants us to come to full maturity in Christ—feeling, thinking, and acting with the character of Jesus as our operating system. Paul will later say in Ephesians 4:13 that various ministry gifts have been given to the body of Christ to serve us "until we all . . . become mature, attaining to the whole measure of the fullness of Christ." There it is again. Being spiritually mature means we have the fullness of Jesus shaping every aspect of our lives.

Your motives. Your attention. Your work. Your play. Your friendships. Your family. Your loves. Your choices. Jesus wants you to be filled and full of him. Full stop.

When your back is turned, may people begin to whisper about you: "She is so full of Jesus," or "He is so full of Christ's love."

Paul's measure is beyond measure, yes. And while there is no ordinary human being that could contain the "measure of all the fullness of God," Jesus can.

The mystery, the miracle that sits at the center of the gospel, is that Jesus lives in you and me (Col. 1:27).

THE PRAYER

Lord Jesus, I am in you and you are in me. I want to be full of you, radiant with you, permeated with you, encompassed by you, mature in you. I believe that because you live in me, I will come to experience what is prayed for me in this prayer. I want to be filled "to the measure of all the fullness of God." In Christ Jesus, I pray, amen.

THE QUESTIONS

- What metaphor most resonates with you when you think of being "full" with all of who God is?

- How could you begin to pray in such a way that you daily welcome God to fill you with his presence?

7

IMMEASURABLY MORE

EPHESIANS 3:14–21

For this reason I kneel before the Father, from whom every family in heaven and on earth derives its name. I pray that out of his glorious riches he may strengthen you with power through his Spirit in your inner being, so that Christ may dwell in your hearts through faith. And I pray that you, being rooted and established in love, may have power, together with all the Lord's holy people, to grasp how wide and long and high and deep is the love of Christ, and to know this love that surpasses knowledge—that you may be filled to the measure of all the fullness of God.

Now to him who is able to do immeasurably more than all we ask or imagine, according to his power that is at work within us, to him be glory in the church and in Christ Jesus throughout all generations, for ever and ever! Amen.

CONSIDER THIS

Have you ever noticed how the punctuation marks in a sentence can radically change its meaning?

Some instances can be quite funny, and you may have seen them. For example: a) See Joe run. b) See Joe? Run! Likewise, a well-chosen punctuation mark that comes at the *end* of a sentence can help us understand the intent of everything that precedes it.

I like to see verses 20–21, the "doxology" of Paul's prayer, as one sentence-long punctuation mark guiding how we are to pray the preceding verses. I know I'm stretching a metaphor, but it's true—how Paul finishes his prayer impacts the meaning of everything that came before. Paul punctuates his prayer—with worship!

Our prayer lives thrive in an atmosphere of worship.

A doxology is a praise-filled acclamation, a declaration that all glory belongs to God. Paul wants to wrap up his prayer with unwavering conviction, proclaiming that the glorious God, who can do anything, will answer.

Let's explore Paul's spiritual punctuation mark on his prayer: "Now to him who is able to do immeasurably more than all we ask or imagine, according to his power that is at work within us, to him be glory in the church and in Christ Jesus throughout all generations, for ever and ever! Amen" (vv. 20–21).

What if we punctuated every one of our prayers like this? What inner trust in God we might build!

Making the prayer our own, in verse 20, we are asking God to bring us into communion with Jesus and an experience of his love—believing he is "able to do immeasurably more than all we ask or imagine." In other words, we know who we are talking to. We don't pray to ourselves, or to one another (though I have heard this done a time or two). We pray to the Creator, the God of the universe, in Jesus's name. With confidence.

Also in verse 20, we declare that God's power is "at work within us." This means that we know we are Spirit-filled and Spirit-empowered people. We're not on our own. Jesus has made his home in us! There is no "maybe God will," or "I hope God will" wishy-washy-ness in Paul's prayer. Nor should there be in ours.

And in verse 21 of Paul's doxology, we come to one of the most important two-word phrases in the New Testament. Paul will use this phrase over and over again in his writing about union with God and experiencing the fullness of love. It is part of his punctuation mark on this prayer.

It is the phrase, "in Christ."

More than one hundred times in his New Testament letters (estimates vary) we see Paul using the phrase "in Christ," or some variation of it (e.g., "in Christ Jesus," "in the Lord Jesus," and others). "In Christ" is Paul's way of talking about our union with, and participation in, the life of Jesus. Being "in Christ" is Paul's way of talking about salvation and the teaching of Jesus in John 14, 15, and 17. While the word *Christian* appears only a handful

     DAN WILT

of times in the New Testament, "in Christ" and its variations fill the pages of Paul's letters.

Next, we will give time to this pivotal phrase we see in the Prayer of Union and Love, and in Paul's New Testament letters. Let's pray together that God would reveal the fullness of its meaning for us as followers of Jesus. Understanding its essential message has everything to do with us flourishing in faith over a lifetime.

THE PRAYER

Lord Jesus, I am in you and you are in me. Teach me to pray with worship and abounding faith, as Paul did. I am ready to turn the "amens" in my prayers to "amens!" I believe; help me in my unbelief (Mark 9:24). And Lord, I want to understand what it means to be "in Christ." Begin now to show me what this means as you live your life through me (Gal. 2:20). In Christ Jesus, I pray, amen.

THE QUESTIONS

- What kinds of prayers are you praying these days?

- If you had to describe your prayers with a punctuation mark, how would you describe them (question mark, period, comma, exclamation mark)?

- What do you think it means to be "in Christ"?

8

IN CHRIST JESUS

EPHESIANS 3:14–21

For this reason I kneel before the Father, from whom every family in heaven and on earth derives its name. I pray that out of his glorious riches he may strengthen you with power through his Spirit in your inner being, so that Christ may dwell in your hearts through faith. And I pray that you, being rooted and established in love, may have power, together with all the Lord's holy people, to grasp how wide and long and high and deep is the love of Christ, and to know this love that surpasses knowledge—that you may be filled to the measure of all the fullness of God.

Now to him who is able to do immeasurably more than all we ask or imagine, according to his power that is at work within us, to him be glory in the church and **in Christ Jesus** throughout all generations, for ever and ever! Amen.

CONSIDER THIS

Have you been slowly memorizing the Prayer of Union and Love in Ephesians 3:14–21? By repeating the entire passage day after day, we are getting it in our hearts and minds. Let's look at one more phrase in verse 21 before we move on—"in Christ Jesus."

Many years ago I visited St. Petersburg, Russia, as part of a team coordinating a national arts festival. On one of our days off, we made our way to an outdoor market where local artisans were selling their crafts. Looking for a gift for my oldest daughter, I was drawn to a set of meticulously painted *matryoshka* dolls—better known as Russian nesting dolls. One doll opens in the middle to reveal another, smaller doll. Then another. Then another, and so on. This goes on until one gets to the smallest doll.

When I read the phrase, "in Christ Jesus," as we see it in verse 21, I often think of those nesting dolls. While it is a limited metaphor (as all metaphors are when talking about big theological ideas), being "in Christ" could be understood to mean we are "inside Christ."

Using the nesting dolls as a simple but helpful visual image, we are nested *inside Christ*—inside his family, inside his heart, inside his promises, inside his covenant faithfulness, inside his righteousness, inside his care, inside his death, inside his resurrection, inside his love. Like many truths of the Scriptures, there is a level of mystery to all this. But it's a beautiful mystery we must explore to embrace all that living in Christ means for us—and for the world God loves (John 3:16).

In its shortest and clearest form, we can understand being "in Christ" as Paul's special way of talking about our union with Jesus—us abiding in Christ (John 15:4–5) and Christ abiding in us (15:4; 17:23).

By the Holy Spirit, Paul expands throughout his letters on all the benefits we experience being in this mutual, abiding relationship—this participation in the life of Jesus.

While we don't want to get too far ahead of ourselves, let's list just a few New Testament ideas that are connected to being "in Christ."

- Being "in Christ" means that Jesus is in us, and we are in Jesus (John 15:4–5; 17:23).
- Being "in Christ" means we are united with Jesus in his death and resurrection, alive to God and dead to sin (Rom. 6:5–11).
- Being "in Christ" means we are united with Jesus, and are one with him in spirit (1 Cor. 6:17).
- Being "in Christ" means that we were included in Jesus when we heard the gospel, believed, and were marked with the seal of the Holy Spirit (Eph. 1:13).
- Being "in Christ" means that we flourish within Jesus's care as we live every aspect of our lives in intimate relationship with him (Acts 17:28).
- Being "in Christ" means we are incorporated into the body of Christ, the family of God. We are joined to

God's people as one body and are the benefactors of his promises (1 Cor. 12:12–27; Gal. 3:28; Eph. 3:6).

- Being "in Christ" means we are "members" of Christ himself (1 Cor. 6:15), united with him and with one another as the body of Christ (Rom. 12:4–5).
- Being "in Christ" means that we are co-heirs with Christ (Rom. 8:17), made alive in the Second Adam, Jesus (1 Cor. 15:22).
- Being "in Christ" means we are not condemned to or by sin; we are free from the law of sin and death and live by the law of the Spirit (Rom. 8:1).
- Being "in Christ" means we are a new creation in him (2 Cor. 5:17).
- Being "in Christ" means that we are reconciled to God; our sins are not counted against us and we have the ministry of reconciliation (2 Cor. 5:18–19).
- Being "in Christ" means that our life is hidden in Jesus and will appear with him in glory (Col. 3:3–4).
- Being "in Christ" means that we are seated with him in heavenly places, experiencing his riches and kindness (Eph. 2:6–7).

And there is so much more to what it means to be in Christ!

We must begin to think differently about who and Whose we are as we move through this world, my brothers and sisters! Who you are, and who I am, is someone who is *in Christ*. As N. T. Wright put it, "It is a strange idea to most of us, but for some a very necessary one; that you might begin again from scratch *to learn who you are*."[6] Let's learn who we are together.

With the words, "to him be glory in the church and in Christ Jesus throughout all generations, for ever and ever! Amen," Paul concludes his Prayer of Union and Love. But how did Paul come to see both his and our relationship with Jesus in this "in Christ" way? We will find some answers in the story of his conversion—coming up next.

THE PRAYER

Lord Jesus, I am in you and you are in me. To live in you, as you live in me, is my heart's desire. Teach me what it means to live "in Christ," and help me to understand all that is our inheritance as those united with you. In Christ Jesus, I pray, amen.

THE QUESTIONS

- Have you ever thought about the phrase, "in Christ"? Do you find the idea of being "inside Christ" helpful, and if so, in what ways?

---

6. N. T. Wright, *Paul for Everyone: Galatians and Thessalonians* (Louisville: Westminster John Knox Press, 2004), 24, emphasis original.

9

THE APOSTLE OF UNION AND LOVE (PART ONE)

ACTS 9:1–9

Meanwhile, Saul was still breathing out murderous threats against the Lord's disciples. He went to the high priest and asked him for letters to the synagogues in Damascus, so that if he found any there who belonged to the Way, whether men or women, he might take them as prisoners to Jerusalem. As he neared Damascus on his journey, suddenly a light from heaven flashed around him. He fell to the ground and heard a voice say to him, "Saul, Saul, why do you persecute me?"

"Who are you, Lord?" Saul asked.

"I am Jesus, whom you are persecuting," he replied. "Now get up and go into the city, and you will be told what you must do."

The men traveling with Saul stood there speechless; they heard the sound but did not see anyone. Saul got up from the ground, but when he opened his eyes he could see nothing. So they led him by the hand into Damascus. For three days he was blind, and did not eat or drink anything.

How does a first-century enemy of Jesus and a murderer of his followers become one of the world's greatest writers on union with Christ and the topic of love?

We first meet Saul in Acts 7:57 as he presides over the martyrdom of Stephen. Then, in Acts 9, we meet Saul again traveling on the road to Damascus to arrest followers of Jesus (he is called Paul in Acts 13:9).

Paul is a leader mid-mission, mid-purpose, mid-stride. He believes he is in the center of his calling, raised up for such a time as this. And there, in the middle of the road, he is halted, arrested, and pulled out of the game. A bright light flashes around him. He is blinded. He is in the dust—in the presence of Jesus.

That is when Jesus reveals his intimate union with the body of Christ. Paul has been persecuting Christians. Jesus asks, "Why do you persecute *me*?" Paul wasn't persecuting Jesus; he was persecuting believers, right? When Paul asks who is the one who is speaking to him, this one who identifies with the believing church, Jesus answers, "I am Jesus, whom you are persecuting." Jesus identifies with his people; his church is in him, and he is in his church.

Given the incredible and prolific writings on love that flow from Paul after this encounter, I would propose we consider this possibility: Paul was not confronted by some generic version of divine power—he was arrested by personal and profound love.

Three insights in Paul's conversion story will help us as we learn how we grow in deeper union, deeper intimacy, with Jesus.

The first insight is this: *Sometimes we have to lose our sight to gain a vision* (v. 9).

Paul trusted in his capacities and his skills as a believer in, and teacher about, God. But sometimes we're blinded by our abilities, passions, talents, learning, or experience. We are blind to an even more beautiful vision of who God truly is. When a cataclysm occurs in our lives, one that makes us wonder if we ever knew God at all, we can be given new sight! We are given the opportunity to gain a fresh vision of God—and the eyes of our humbled hearts are opened to perceive him in a new way (Eph. 1:18–21).

The second insight is this: *Sometimes we have to lose our time to gain eternity* (v. 9; Gal. 1:11–24).

After Paul's encounter and some initial ministry, according to Galatians 1, it seems he disappears from the scene for three years to learn the gospel—by revelation—from Jesus. In seasons of transformation, God puts us on his timetable, and he is in no hurry. We begin to measure in long-time, trust-time, wait-time, and growth-time. Sometimes we have to lose time, by our perception, to gain eternity in our hearts (Eccl. 3:11).

The third insight is this: *Sometimes we have to lose our job to gain a mission—or rather, for a mission to gain us.*

Sometimes we have to lose what we thought we were engaged by God to do in order to be enlisted in a fresh mission with God. Paul thought he knew who he was, what he was about, what he was *for*. He thought he understood so much about the nature of God and his purposes. And in a flash, a moment in time, his job, his task, his business card, his metrics for success and achievement and value, were removed from him. Jesus, and his mission to love the world to himself, became the new mission of the apostle Paul.

Paul's business card was rewritten in the middle of that road; Beloved Son was all that was left written on it. And from that sense of union with the Lord who loved him enough to stop him, free him, and change him, from that abounding sense of beginning "to know this love" (Eph. 3:19) that God had for him (1 John 4:16), Paul was set on a new course that has reached us today.

God turns our greatest losses into our greatest gains (Phil. 3:7–8). Paul, now "in Christ," was loved to life by Jesus himself.

THE PRAYER

Lord Jesus, I am in you and you are in me. I thank you that my perceived losses of sight, time, and mission can lead me to a greater knowledge of you and your love for me. Use each one of my difficult seasons to bring me the gain of knowing you (Phil. 3:7–8). In Christ Jesus, I pray, amen.

THE QUESTIONS

- Have you experienced, in some season of your life, a loss? Perhaps you felt you lost your spiritual sight, an opportunity, or sense of purpose?

- What would happen if you began to see each loss as a doorway that leads to the gain of knowing Jesus more fully?

10

THE APOSTLE OF UNION AND LOVE (PART TWO)

GALATIANS 1:11–12

I want you to know, brothers and sisters, that the gospel I preached is not of human origin. I did not receive it from any man, nor was I taught it; rather, I received it by revelation from Jesus Christ.

CONSIDER THIS

A good friend of mine is a health coach. Sometimes we sit down together over coffee (a matcha latte with unsweetened almond milk, in my case), and I never fail to learn something new. My friend often reminds me that becoming healthy is not only about learning new ways of caring for my body and mind. It is also about unlearning old ways I have treated my body and mind—ways that may have seemed right and natural but ultimately led to a lack of health. For me to get healthier, he says, some old ways of thinking, some old habits, will have to die.

I imagine that Paul had plenty of learning and unlearning to do when Jesus met him on the road to Damascus in Acts 9. There Paul was, lying in the dust, in the presence of the risen Jesus. His mind was probably racing to match this revelatory experience he was having with everything he had studied about God all his life in the Old Testament Scriptures. In a grand, sweeping reframe, the kind that only a revelation from the Spirit can bring, Paul was seeing everything he knew about God and his people in a new light.

And that's what revelation from the Holy Spirit does—it surprises us, takes us off guard, and schools us in a new way of seeing the world. We see old things we once knew coming back to us with new life. We see old ways we were clinging to needing to die. We see truths we had never seen before with delight and gratefulness. With the written Word of God as our guide, the Holy Spirit delights to gift us with special and very personal moments of insight, of epiphany, of revelation—as the Spirit guides us into all truth (John 16:13) through the changing seasons of our lives.

In Galatians 1:11–12, Paul declares that everything he knew about the gospel (which includes how God relates to us and how we relate to God) he learned by revelation from Jesus. All the stories he held dear about God's covenant bond with Israel, about God's *hesed* (loyal, unwavering, steadfast) covenant love toward

Israel, were reframed by this encounter with Jesus. He would go on to write from the heart of this revelation from Jesus in the letters of the New Testament. Passages like our Prayer of Union and Love in Ephesians 3:14–21 shine from within with the teaching of Jesus. Paul learned about our union with God in Christ and about the nature of God's love toward us from Jesus himself.

So should we.

I believe we live in a constant need for Jesus to school us, time and time again, in what it means to live in union with him and within the bonds of new covenant love. For example, when we imagine God to be distant and outside of us as we pray, to be pleaded with and begged to move on our behalf, are we missing what it means to have the Spirit of Jesus and his love indwelling us? Do we quietly put Jesus at arm's length in our worship services out of our insecurity about what it might mean if we embraced his invitation—as a local church—to participate in the love and life of the Trinity (John 17:20–23)?

I know that I have some learning and unlearning to do about being united with Christ and about what real love actually means. I believe that, like Paul, we all need fresh moments of revelation from Jesus along the way to shake us and wake us from our spiritual slumber. We need Jesus to meet us in our wrestling, to reveal old, unhelpful ways of thinking about God's work within us that are ultimately impeding our spiritual health.

I, for one, am ready to learn again at the feet of Jesus. Paul got his ideas about being "in Christ," and about the nature of love in 1 Corinthians 13, by revelation from Jesus himself. With a humble heart and a willingness to learn, we'll now turn our attention toward Jesus's teachings in the Gospel of John so we might better understand what he means when he says, "I am in my Father, and you are in me, and I am in you" (John 14:20).

THE PRAYER

Lord Jesus, I am in you and you are in me. I thank you for how kindly you have revealed yourself to me through the years and taught me new things about your heart for me and your love for me. I am ready to learn at your feet. Teach me. In Christ Jesus, I pray, amen.

THE QUESTIONS

- Can you remember a moment when the Holy Spirit revealed to you something you needed to learn?

- Can you remember a moment when the Spirit revealed to you something you needed to unlearn?

- How are you different because of those revelations?

11

WITNESSES OF UNION AND LOVE

LUKE 10:21

At that time Jesus, full of joy through the Holy Spirit, said, "I praise you, Father, Lord of heaven and earth, because you have hidden these things from the wise and learned, and revealed them to little children. Yes, Father, for this is what you were pleased to do."

ACTS 1:8b

"You will be my witnesses in Jerusalem, and in all Judea and Samaria, and to the ends of the earth."

CONSIDER THIS

Today, we prepare to enter the School of Union and Love with Jesus, our teacher—the Lord of Union and Love.

To do that, we need to pause, slow our pace, and consider how disciples have postured themselves for learning from Jesus for millennia. If we know what our teacher's goal is for us as students, then we know how best to position ourselves for growth.

In the coming days, we are going to sit at the feet of Jesus in the Gospel of John, particularly chapters 14, 15, and 17, to learn from our Rabbi and Master. We will learn what it means to live "in Christ," and how Jesus intends to love us and others through us in our day-to-day lives. Just as Paul did, just as Mary did, just as all the disciples did—we will invite the Holy Spirit to open our hearts, revealing to us the precious and deep things of God.

And what is Jesus's goal in our learning, even through a daily reflection like this? The goal of the Lord of Union and Love is to train *witnesses*, not just students, for extending his loving ministry in the world. As my friend J. D. Walt says, "A witness is a disciple on fire." A student, even a disciple, may falter—but a witness is *unstoppable*. A witness encounters Christ's love, is changed by that encounter, and then bears witness to that encounter to the world God loves (John 3:16).

And the only appropriate posture for becoming a witness, according to Jesus, is to come to him as a child (Matt. 18:2–3). Children are open—open to growing, open to learning, and open to mimicking and becoming like the one who is teaching them. Paul had to become like a child on the road to Damascus, humbled and ready to learn, from Jesus himself, what union with God in Christ was all about.

In John 3, Jesus is speaking to the astute and highly studied religious leader, Nicodemus. Nicodemus knows the Hebrew Scriptures inside and out. He is smart and knowledgeable. But he comes to Jesus as a student. He comes tender and curious. We can almost sense his child-like heart in the text. Jesus baffles him by saying he must be "born again" (John 3:3), born of the flesh and born of the Spirit. Nicodemus would need to lay down all he had known before in order to become like a child *before* he could fully experience what Jesus was teaching.

Come like a child.

That's the way the Lord of Union and Love trains *witnesses*. He starts by inviting us to come with innocence, openness, trust, and expectation. From that posture, what he reveals can be absorbed, applied, and lived.

In Luke 10:21 Jesus is filled with joy about this learning posture in his apprentices. "At that time Jesus, full of joy through the Holy Spirit, said, 'I praise you, Father, Lord of heaven and earth, because you have hidden these things from the wise and learned, and revealed them to little children. Yes, Father, for this is what you were pleased to do.'"

He then says to Nicodemus a few words about being a witness of God's works: "Very truly I tell you, we speak of what we know, and we testify to what we have seen . . ." (John 3:11). In other words: "Become like a child, Nicodemus. Be born of the Spirit and start again, start new, in me. Become a witness of what God is doing right before your eyes."

And that is why there is no use running just another Bible study about being united with Christ and experiencing the love of God. In the school of Jesus, there is only usefulness in running a witness study. Witnesses see, experience, and apply what they are learning. Please hear me, studying the Bible plays a huge part in us becoming discipled witnesses of what Jesus can do in and through us. But if Bible study is the extent of our discipleship, then the written Word of God, left unapplied, remains unbelieved.

Jesus is not interested in simply educating and informing us about how to "know this love that surpasses knowledge" and how to live in "all the fullness of God" (Eph. 3:19). Jesus is not interested in giving us lectures, reviewing the material, and then serving up a test on what we have come to know about abiding in Christ.

The early disciples heard Jesus's teaching, but they also witnessed Jesus living in union with the Father, the Spirit moving through him. They became Witnesses of Union and Love. They saw the power of love that flowed from that Trinitarian intimacy and mission. They wanted to be a part of that family, that relational community, that new way of life (Acts 5:20).

And because they saw that new life in living color, in Jesus, they could bear testimony to it. Apprenticing alongside Jesus, applying his teaching in real-time with real feedback, they became his trained witnesses (Acts 1:8). They even became the unified body, united "in heart and mind," just as Jesus had prayed (John 17:21–24; Acts 4:32). They practiced what they preached about being in one accord with Jesus, and in one accord with one another (Acts 2:1; 4:32–35).

So I want to welcome you to become a witness through what we will discover in the teaching of Jesus over these next days. Ask Jesus to apply every insight to your life, and then lean in, moment by moment, each day. His goal is that we would become his apprentices, his witnesses—those who live like he lives, love like he loves, and do what he does in our homes and neighborhoods (Luke 11:28).

With our Prayer of Union and Love from Ephesians 3:14–21 in our hearts (feel free to pray it every morning as we continue), and with the story of Paul's conversion in Acts 9 before us (as he became the Apostle of Union and Love), we now enter the School of Union and Love with the Lord of Union and Love—to become Witnesses of Union and Love.

We will do this all in the presence of Jesus.

THE PRAYER

Lord Jesus, I am in you and you are in me. I come as a little child, ready to learn all you would have me to learn, and to experience all you would want me to experience. I want to be a disciple on fire, a true witness of what it means to live in you and have you live in and through me. In Christ Jesus, I pray, amen.

THE QUESTIONS

- Are you ready to become a witness, a true "disciple on fire" of Jesus?

- How could you posture yourself, like Paul, to learn at the feet of Jesus and apply his teaching?

- What adult attitudes might you need to put off, and what childlike attitudes might you need to put on?

12

JESUS INVITES US TO HIS IN-CROWD

JOHN 14:10–11, 20

"Don't you believe that I am in the Father, and that the Father is in me? The words I say to you I do not speak on my own authority. Rather, it is the Father, living in me, who is doing his work. Believe me when I say that I am in the Father and the Father is in me; or at least believe on the evidence of the works themselves."

"On that day you will realize that I am in my Father, and you are in me, and I am in you."

CONSIDER THIS

Did you have an in-crowd in your high school? If so, do you remember how it seemed as though many of your classmates were endlessly thinking about who was in and who was out? If we weren't talking about it, whispering about it in the stands of a football game or the back of math class, many of us were preoccupied with thinking about our place in the social pecking order.

The in-crowd represented not only popularity, being liked, or feeling appreciated. The in-crowd also represented the idea that someone might see us, know us, value us, love us—for who we were. For those of us who felt like we were on the outside, looking in on someone's else's in-crowd, we often created our own.

If you found your people, a friend or friend group that was healthy and truly did *see* you, *know* you, *value* you, and *love* you for who you were, then it felt like you had found your place in the world. With that little group of friends, you felt at home, you were part of one another, and you moved as one.

Jesus came to put us all in the in-crowd with the Trinity. And this passage is where that story finds its source. If you are a follower of Jesus, my brother, my sister—*you are in the in-crowd.*

In John 14:10–11, 20, we see Jesus addressing his disciples with a question: "Don't you believe that I am in the Father, and that the Father is in me?"

"Yes," they may have answered sheepishly, knowing their answer was probably right—though it could be a trick question.

Jesus continued:

"The words I say to you I do not speak on my own authority. Rather, it is the Father, living in me, who is doing his work. Believe me when I say that I am in the Father and the Father is in me; or at least believe on the evidence of the works themselves."

Surely this teaching must have been shocking when the disciples first heard it. They would have quickly recalled the moment in John 10:30 when Jesus told the teachers of the law, right there in front of God and everyone in the temple courts, "I and the Father are one." Hearts stopped. Stones were picked up. Faces flushed red with anger and disbelief. They accused him of blaspheming, of claiming to be God.

Now, in John 14, Jesus is saying it again, only to the disciples in private.

Jesus wanted them, and wants us, to understand an essential truth of the faith: When we see Jesus, we see the heart of the Father (John 14:8–9). Jesus and the Father are one. This is Jesus saying he has made his home in the Father, and the Father has made his home in Jesus. It is a special, Trinitarian relationship with the Spirit that cannot be replicated. The Trinity is a divine union unto itself.

But then an in-crowd twist comes in verse 20: "On that day you will realize that I am in my Father, and you are in me, and I am in you."

Wait. Jesus, did you just include *us* in the in-crowd?

 DAN WILT

Let's be honest. We can sometimes get confused when Jesus talks like this. Yes, we understand there is mystery to all of this, but what exactly is he saying? Just how "in" are we?

Some italics may help us here. Jesus *did not* say that we *are* Jesus or the Father; Jesus said we are *in* Jesus who is *in* the Father. Jesus *did not* say that Jesus *is* us; he said Jesus is *in* us. There is a big difference here. As an old adage goes, "There is a God. You are not him." However, we are invited to share life together with Jesus—intimate, relational life—being at home in one another, moving as one.

This is the language of relationship, abiding, and communion. It is the language of sharing, participation, and being embraced by divine love.

And here's the very big deal for all those who have ever felt on the outside looking in with God's love.

According to Jesus—as his follower, you are in the in-crowd with the Trinity! We are full participants in the life and love that exists within the community of the Father, Son, and Holy Spirit. We retain our distinction, yes, but we are part of that family, part of that communion, part of that fellowship that exists between Father, Son, and Holy Spirit.

We are on the inside of the in-crowd with Jesus—and we are looking outward to bring others in along the way! We will bear witness to his indwelling presence, his incomparable love, until everyone who is outside, or feels outside, is inside his community of grace.

Today, know that you are accepted. You are seen. You are known. You are valued. You are loved. You are an insider, within the love of Jesus. If you ever felt like an outsider, misunderstood, and not appreciated, let this be the day of your liberation. You have found your people—and have been found by your God.

THE PRAYER

Lord Jesus, I am in you and you are in me. I am just beginning to understand how loved and accepted I am by you. I can be hard on myself, but knowing that you value me even in my worst moments is a healing balm to my soul. Reveal to me how much you love me, and how completely in the circle of your love I truly am. In Christ Jesus, I pray, amen.

THE QUESTIONS

- Have you ever taken the time to think about what it means to be in the in-crowd with the Trinity?

- Do you feel like you could ever consider God distant again, knowing this truth?

13

ABIDING IN THE VINE

JOHN 15:4–5, 9

"Remain in me, as I also remain in you. No branch can bear fruit by itself; it must remain in the vine. Neither can you bear fruit unless you remain in me. I am the vine; you are the branches. If you remain in me and I in you, you will bear much fruit; apart from me you can do nothing."

"As the Father has loved me, so have I loved you. Now remain in my love."

CONSIDER THIS

Every morning my wife, without fail, finds her way into our family room. As I hear the door quietly shut behind her, I know what she is about to do. She is about to sit at the feet of the Lord of Union and Love, Jesus, just as Mary did (Luke 10:39). My wife goes into that place of meeting for one reason—to strengthen her abiding in Jesus as the day begins.

As we sit at the feet of Jesus in the Gospel of John, we can see that Jesus is a master teacher. He rarely draws on metaphors that have only one meaning, or only make sense in his time and place. He is often drawing on imagery that would have been penetrating to his audience, faithful Jews, who knew their Old Testament inside and out.

The image of the vine and the branches is one of those images. In Psalm 80:7–11, the people of Israel are described as a vine, planted by God. In Isaiah 5:1–7, Israel is described as a vine that has produced grapes unfit for eating. In Jewish thought, Israel is thought to be the vine, and the vineyard, of God.

Then, the Lord of Union and Love comes on the scene.

"I am the vine," Jesus says. His disciples pause. He is saying that he is the true Israel. He will carry God's desires to fulfillment through loving obedience where Israel had failed. He is simultaneously saying something very personal to his followers—that if his disciples abide *in* him, live *in* him, stay *in* him, and remain connected to him as their source of life, they will bear good, sweet, and lasting fruit.

Then Jesus goes on in verse 9 to add: "As the Father has loved me, so have I loved you. Now remain in my love."

In union with Jesus, dwelling in the vine of his person and presence, we experience the fullness of love. Making our home in Christ, and having Christ make his home in us, is both life-giving and love-renewing. Jesus is communicating to his followers the importance of staying connected to him, like a branch living in symbiotic harmony with the vine from which it springs.

There are a few insights here for us. A branch is of the same plant as the vine. They are one. A branch is connected to, and is an expression of, the vine. The vine and branch participate in a shared life. A branch is fully integrated into the vine as its source of life, renewal, and replenishment. A branch of a grapevine bears fruit that is of the same ilk as the vine. They share the same DNA. The vine and the branch are intimately and purposefully joined.

And if a branch, heaven forbid (and I mean that), ever decides it can live apart from its vine—we know how that story ends. A branch disconnected from a source of life withers, becomes brittle, and eventually dies.

In John 15:4–5, the word translated "remain" or "abide"—*meno*—is a word that also means "stay."

Jesus is saying, "*Stay* in me. We are connected; you are not designed to live apart from my presence and love." We as human beings can resist all we want; health waits on the other side of staying, remaining, and abiding in the source of Jesus. And when times get hard, and we want to look to other sources for love, for affirmation, for encouragement, for salvation—Jesus says, "Stay."

My wife is moved to pray each morning because she must. She knows the challenges that may come that day. She is praying to abide; she is abiding so she can remain present to the love of Jesus. "Prayer, or as Jesus called it, 'abiding,' can no longer mean speaking words to a deity somewhere out there. It must mean walking and talking with the God who is both transcendently present 'at the right hand of God the Father Almighty,' and imminently by our side, closer than our breath. Indeed, this is pure mystery and yet it is the ultimate and immediate reality."[7]

Staying in Christ, not moving from him, is a state of the heart renewed by consistent prayer, by worship, and by lingering in God's Word and God's presence. "As the Father has loved me, so have I loved you. Now remain in my love," means that we have the privilege of participating—fully—in the shared life between the Father and the Son, by the Holy Spirit.

Stay in Jesus. "Prone to wander, Lord, I feel it, prone to leave the God I love" goes the old hymn.[8] *Stay in union with him—do whatever it takes.* Your source will never fail you.

---

7. J. D. Walt, *Right Here Right Now, Jesus: Moving from a Prayer Life to a Life of Prayer* (Franklin, TN: Seedbed Publishing, 2019), 44–45.
8. "Come Thou Fount of Every Blessing," lyrics by Robert Robinson (1758).

THE PRAYER

Lord Jesus, I am in you and you are in me. There is no other source for me that matches my need; if I am a branch of the vine, then I choose to remain in you, daily, to draw my strength from you as my source. I choose to stay where I will thrive most in love — in intimate relationship with you. In Christ Jesus, I pray, amen.

THE QUESTIONS

- How are you doing at staying, remaining, in Jesus as your source of life and growth?

- What could you do to stay in him as the pressures of life seek to separate you?

14

AS I HAVE LOVED YOU

JOHN 15:12–13

"My command is this: Love each other as I have loved you. Greater love has no one than this: to lay down one's life for one's friends."

CONSIDER THIS

Being like Jesus can be just plain *hard*. In my pastoral work, I've spent a lot of time over the years with people struggling with a challenging relationship, or processing a relationship in which they feel a separation has emerged. Inevitably, many of those conversations have ended up in a similar place. To break the cycle, one of the two people must act like Jesus. Someone will have to love that other person as Jesus would—sacrificially, consistently, and with no expectation of return.

In virtually every case, the person has balked. I understand why because I've felt the same hesitation myself. "I'm not Jesus! How in the world will I be able to love this person unconditionally who is acting so poorly toward me?" On your own, you can't. But Jesus, loving through you, can.

Jesus is a rubber-meets-the-road kind of Rabbi in the School of Union and Love. One moment, we're sitting at his feet, enjoying all the comforts that come with knowing we are seen, known, valued, and loved. Then Jesus says words like this in John 15:12–13 and things get *real*: "My command is this: Love each other as I have loved you. Greater love has no one than this: to lay down one's life for one's friends."

"Love each other . . ." Okay, Lord. I will love my brothers and my sisters to the very best of my ability. But if I do my best, and I can't pull it off, I know you'll understand. I'll call it a day (and I may, perhaps, talk to others about why I couldn't handle their broken attitude and failure of discipleship). But then I'll move on—reluctantly, of course.

But Jesus won't let us leave off the second part of his sentence. He waits for us to read it and to really comprehend its meaning: "Love each other . . . as I have loved you." And how have you loved us, Jesus?

Completely. Fully. Without reservation. Through it all. Through trouble. Through misunderstanding. Through fear. Through disobedience. You stay. You love. You heal from within the mess—not from outside of it.

"As I have loved you" can mean only one thing. I must be willing to die, in a hundred small ways, for my brother or sister. That is how we love. That is how I am to love my brother and sister. (I would note that I don't believe that this passage means we *always* need to stay in a hard situation with a fellow Christian or fellow Christians. But I do believe we need to continue to love and forgive our brother or sister in Christ through it.)

In the real world, this feels like emotional rocket science. Laying down my life for another, especially when I've been hurt by them, is difficult.

- Laying down my need for that person to humble themselves first and ask for my forgiveness?
- Laying down my time when it's inconvenient?
- Laying down my opinions when I'm sure I'm right?
- Laying down my reputation to stand beside someone who made a mistake and needs my support?
- Laying down my anger against someone who hurt me?
- Laying down my efforts to build my own kingdom and care for my own circle above all others?
- Laying down my need to hoard what I perceive to be *my* resources to make sure I always have enough?

These are challenging questions for all of us.

Jesus sees. Jesus knows. And this one thing he knows above all. We cannot love each other as he has loved us—without him loving others through us.

Christ in us can love people through us—as he has loved us. Living in union with him, we can get there from here.

Peter heard what Jesus said and wrote these words: "Now that you have purified yourselves by obeying the truth so that you have sincere love for each other, love one another deeply, from the heart" (1 Peter 1:22).

We can only love as expansively as Jesus loves because the Holy Spirit is in us, and will help us. *Jesus, help us love one another today as you have loved us.*

THE PRAYER

Lord Jesus, I am in you and you are in me. There is a story of your unified church in our generation of which I want to be a part. Teach me how you want me to love those brothers and sisters in my circle of relationships. I want to learn how to lay my life down for each one. In Christ Jesus, I pray, amen.

THE QUESTIONS

- How could you prepare your heart for the next challenge you might face with a fellow believer or believers?

- How has Jesus loved you, and how does the "as I have loved you" principle apply to your life?

15

THAT ALL OF THEM MAY BE ONE (PART ONE)

JOHN 17:20–21

"My prayer is not for them alone. I pray also for those who will believe in me through their message, that all of them may be one, Father, just as you are in me and I am in you. May they also be in us so that the world may believe that you have sent me."

CONSIDER THIS

In the ancient world, rulers would put statues of themselves in lands they had conquered to communicate their sovereignty over that people. Each statue, an icon of the ruler, assured everyone when they gazed at it that they were under the care and protection of that master.

In Genesis 1:27, when we see God make man and woman "in his image" to populate the earth, the connection to the ancient practice is clear. We are the "icons,"

God's image-bearers, reflecting his care into the world he loves (John 3:16). Made in God's image, wherever we are as human beings, we are a reminder to one another that we are designed to live—*fully alive*—under the care, protection, and love of the sovereign God.

For we who have said yes to living in union with God in Christ, yes to the covenant invitation of the Father, we carry Jesus—our sovereign—within. As we mature in Christ, increasingly our eyes, our words, and our actions communicate to all: You are loved. You are cared for. You, and all who are in this beautiful world, belong to God. We shine like stars (Phil. 2:15) to the glory of God and for the winning of hearts to him.

Today's passage reminds us that when Jesus makes his habitation in us (John 14:23), as individuals and as a community, together we become remarkable evidence to the world that God is truly love (1 John 4:16). When we live together in unity (Ps. 133:1–3), there is a blessing that follows! Our unified love and selfless caring become powerful evidence that God is truly among us!

As the communion of the saints, as the Apostles' Creed puts it, we are glimpses of God's heart in the world. We are the evidence that God is with us. The credibility of that evidence will always be at stake because it matters so much. Our unity as believers is always a point of frontal attack on the body of Christ in every generation. Our oneness will always be contested.

But we remain the evidence of God's love to the world. For this reason, we must fight for love.

And we must remember this as we do. The unity and love of the people of Jesus over the millennia have been the reason for myriad souls to come to a saving relationship with Jesus. Lives have been transformed! Family lines have been healed! Prisoners have been set free! We need to start watching the real news about the impact of our unity and love as the church through whom Christ lives and acts. We must rehearse that unity among ourselves, and model it in the public sphere rather than staring at all the times we have failed. Our unity lapses shouldn't be our incessant point of conversation.

Yes, we must lament our seasons of disunity. But let the world see us fighting for love! Let's learn from our mistakes and move forward. We must celebrate our unity, demonstrate our unity, rehearse our unity—and do so with public joy! A fixation on our disunified moments has a negative impact on the body of Christ over time. To say it with candor and love, to myself and to the family of Jesus, complaining is easier to do than giving ourselves to the faithful work of healing. And we want to press on to take hold of that for which Christ Jesus took hold of us (Phil. 3:12–14), yes?

That's who we are. That's what we do.

And this is why the Enemy goes after our unity. If the adversary can break the bond of *koinonia* (fellowship) between us, he can render our evangelism impotent and our love diminished in credibility. We become a weak signal to the world God loves (John 3:16).

But here, in this verse, is our hope! Jesus is in us, and has prayed for us! And though our love for one another may be imperfect, it's definitely worth fighting for every time it is contested. Don't give up, and don't hold back. Jesus will bless us in our work for unity—that his peace may rule and reign in our hearts, together as one (Col. 3:15).

THE PRAYER

Lord Jesus, I am in you and you are in me. I want to celebrate the unity of your church and be a part of healing whenever that unity has been broken. May we be one as you and the Father are one—that the world may see you are truly among us. In Christ Jesus, I pray, amen.

THE QUESTIONS

- What posture of the heart is the Lord inviting you to as you pursue unity in the communities of Jesus of which you are a part?

- How can you be a sign of God's unifying love in your church and relationships?

THAT ALL OF THEM MAY BE ONE (PART TWO)

JOHN 17:22–23

"I have given them the glory that you gave me, that they may be one as we are one—I in them and you in me—so that they may be brought to complete unity. Then the world will know that you sent me and have loved them even as you have loved me."

CONSIDER THIS

Are you a lover of group projects? If you are, bless you! If you're not, the line forms behind me. I have been an avid "Oh please, oh please, don't make this a group project!" person ever since I was in grade school. I always ended up doing most of the project, until, of course, the night before it was due. Then, inevitably, a few of my group mates would decide they had something to add (in order to feel good about their participation). The whole presentation would fall apart before my very eyes.

Here is what I've come to realize, however. While I might prefer to do a school project on my own, I definitely don't want to do life on my own. Hundreds of times brothers and sisters, shining with the glory of God in their eyes, have ministered grace and peace to me in Jesus's name.

I've been in need, and they have prayed for me. I've been sick, and they have cared for me. I've been afraid, and they have given me courage. I have needed insight, and they have given me wisdom. I've needed grace, and they have extended it. There have been bumps along the way, but I have never lost my deep love for the body of Christ. We belong to one another (Rom. 12:5), and we need each other to grow into Christlikeness as we navigate the challenges of life.

Just as we are given to one another for support, so, too, we are given to one another to grow in grace. And nothing grows us in grace like *relationships*. You can probably think of a few grace-growers in your own life. I can think of a few people for whom I am a grace-grower in theirs. While some relationships within the church can be hard, they are ultimately vehicles through which Christ is formed in us (Gal. 4:19).

Paul, the Apostle of Union and Love, affirms our part in the work of unity—work that Jesus in us enables us to do, and that changes us as we do it:

Make every effort to keep the unity of the Spirit through the bond of peace. There is one body and one

Spirit, just as you were called to one hope when you were called; one Lord, one faith, one baptism; one God and Father of all, who is over all and through all and in all. (Eph. 4:3–6)

Make every effort. Let's cut straight to it. We can be separated organizationally, and still remain one in love. We can either make every effort to join Jesus in nurturing the "unity of the Spirit through the bond of peace" between us, or we can fall back into the hellish and chaotic separation habits that the world stews in every single day. I, for one, do not want to go back there. I've seen how the world's free-form animosity tears at souls and destroys people's humanity over time. The distorted visions of unity so common to this world, usually based on ideological agreement or blind sentimentality, pale in comparison to the unity into which Christ calls us.

Jesus and his way of sacrificial, cruciform love is the *only* way to complete unity in heart and mind. In the School of Union and Love, John 17:20–23 is our reminder that Jesus prayed for us, as believers, about this. He knew that maintaining unity would be hard work, even with him living in us. And there is no prayer more powerful than a Jesus prayer, the most righteous human being who ever lived (James 5:16).

The Lord of Union and Love then says these words in John 17:23b: "Then the world will know that you sent me and have loved them even as you have loved me."

As a Community of Union and Love, doing all we can to nurture healthy relationships through Christ's power working in us (Col. 1:29), we can become a sign and a wonder to a hurting world. Our relationships, especially with those who are part of the body of Christ, must be fought for, worked for, and pursued with spiritual endurance. We can stop furthering disunity through social media posts and backroom conversations where we malign one another over our differences. It is not to be this way with us. Instead, we can affirm the best, disagree in love and with respect, and work toward unity.

Jesus is here to help us be united in love—to be one as he and the Father are one.

THE PRAYER

Lord Jesus, I am in you and you are in me. I want to make every effort to keep the "unity of the Spirit through the bond of peace" (Eph. 4:3). Show me how I can do my part. In Christ Jesus, I pray, amen.

THE QUESTIONS

- Have you ever experienced unity between believers being a catalyst for someone to come to Jesus? What happened, and what can we learn from that experience?

JESUS MAKES THE FATHER'S LOVE KNOWN TO US

JOHN 17:26

"I have made you known to them, and will continue to make you known in order that the love you have for me may be in them and that I myself may be in them."

CONSIDER THIS

Several years ago some colleagues and I were touring Europe with a group of graduate students. I remember the day our little group walked into the Pantheon in Rome. The word *pantheon* means "of all gods." While the historic purpose of the building is contested, when one walks in and sees the huge concrete dome and *oculus*, a circular window to the sky, it inspires a sense of awe. I remember thinking: *So many gods to please. So little time.*

Can you imagine? It must have been exhausting to worship so many unpredictable gods at once. Jupiter having a bad day is bad news—for everyone.

The God revealed to us in Jesus—the Creator, the Father—is not moody or fickle (James 1:17). In fact, he is the very embodiment of love in its purest form (1 John 4:8). In John 17:26b, Jesus is speaking to the Father, with whom he is one. He says that he is making the Father known for a particular reason: "that the love you have for me may be in them and that I myself may be in them."

"That *the love you have for me* may be in them."

We don't want to miss what's happening here. The Lord of Union and Love is taking us to school again on what it means to be his witnesses in the world he loves (John 3:16).

The Father loves Jesus with a particular *quality* of love. Jesus wants the quality of that love to be *in* us. While the unfathomable quality of the Father's divine love for Jesus may be beyond us, any parent who holds a child in their arms has begun to know at least one aspect of this love. Parental love, in its highest form, cares more deeply for that child than one's own life. Every time I even see a picture of one of my children, my heart fills up. I would do anything for them. They are mine, and I am theirs. We are bonded in ways I will never be bonded with another human soul.

The Father has this kind of love for the Son, though it is deeper and wider and more expansive in its tenderness and affection than you or I could ever imagine.

It is this quality of love that Jesus embodies in the Gospels. In his baptismal waters, when the Father speaks, "This is my Son, whom I love; with him I am well pleased" (Matt. 3:17), Jesus is baptized in this kind of love. No force on earth could ever take that Trinitarian bond of love with the Father and the Spirit away from him. The Father's love is settling, satisfying, fulfilling, and unmatched.

Jesus lives in that love, and the Father's love lives in him. And that is why Jesus is the most compelling person who has ever lived. He embodied the Father's love. Amidst all the small "g" gods of history, not one is the pure embodiment of love. Only the Father is pure love, a quality of love revealed to us in Jesus (Col. 1:15).

Through Jesus, we are awakened to the Father's love. Jesus makes the Father and his love *known*. And experiencing the Father's love embodied in Christ, according to verse 26, we find a desire rising in us to experience that love, to be one with that love, and have it take up residence within us.

Jesus in us is the Father's love in us. Followers of Jesus are the bearers of the Father's transcendent quality of love to the world. "They will know we are Christians by our love," goes the old song. If today you find yourself unsure how to respond to someone, try this:

Be the love of the Father to them.

It is in you to do so, because Jesus—the embodiment of the Father's love—is in you.

THE PRAYER

Lord Jesus, I am in you and you are in me. I want to know the love of the Father. By your presence in me, Jesus, let me be the love of the Father to all those who cross my path today. I want "to know this love" (Eph. 3:19) you have for me, and to share it with all I meet. In Christ Jesus, I pray, amen.

THE QUESTIONS

- Have you ever had an experience of the Father's love for you? How did that experience impact your life?

- How could you show that same love and goodness to others?

REVIEW DAY IN THE SCHOOL OF UNION AND LOVE

1 JOHN 4:16

And so we know and rely on the love God has for us. God is love. Whoever lives in love lives in God, and God in them.

CONSIDER THIS

Review days in school were days to pause, catch our breath, and revisit some of the essential learnings of the past season. Without times of review, we can become too occupied swallowing fresh information rather than taking the time to savor and apply what we've learned. It is in the savoring that learning sticks.

Today we'll take a few moments to review all we have considered in our series so far and to build our anticipation for what is ahead.

We began by immersing ourselves in Ephesians 3:14–21, what we are calling the "Prayer of Union and Love." It is the foundational passage for all we are learning together. Let's read it again, out loud, to get it set in our hearts and to continue to memorize it:

> *For this reason I kneel before the Father, from whom every family in heaven and on earth derives its name. I pray that out of his glorious riches he may strengthen you with power through his Spirit in your inner being, so that Christ may dwell in your hearts through faith. And I pray that you, being rooted and established in love, may have power, together with all the Lord's holy people, to grasp how wide and long and high and deep is the love of Christ, and to know this love that surpasses knowledge—that you may be filled to the measure of all the fullness of God.*
>
> *Now to him who is able to do immeasurably more than all we ask or imagine, according to his power that is at work within us, to him be glory in the church and in Christ Jesus throughout all generations, for ever and ever! Amen.*

The centerpiece of this prayer is found in verse 19, in the little phrase "to know this love." Embracing that Jesus dwells in our hearts through faith—that we are living in union with him—opens the door to us experiencing and knowing the love that Jesus has for us.

Paul, our Apostle of Union and love, writes this incredible prayer from his own experience of God's love in Jesus (Acts 9:1–17; Gal. 2:20b). His understanding of the mystery of the gospel—which he will say is "Christ in you, the hope of glory" (Col. 1:27)—he has learned by revelation from Jesus himself (Gal. 1:12). His language for talking about being a follower of Christ will be summed up in a two-word phrase (and variations of it) that will fill the pages of the New Testament. That phrase is "in Christ."

As Paul learned from Jesus himself what he understood the gospel to be, we are now going with the Lord of Union and Love, Jesus, into the School of Union and Love, his teaching—primarily in John 14, 15, and 17.

Learning at the feet of Jesus, we are unpacking his words related to union with himself (him in us and us in him) and love. We are doing this because the ideas of union with Christ and his "love that surpasses knowledge" (Eph. 3:19) are inseparable. To experience one is to experience the other. Union with God in Christ is not only the goal of every human life, it is also the relational trajectory of the entire Bible.

And where is all this going? Learning at the feet of Jesus, and opening ourselves to his Spirit dwelling within us, we are becoming Witnesses of Union and Love. We are becoming witnesses who share what we have experienced.

      DAN WILT

The world will see Jesus because they are meeting us—his witnesses in whom he dwells and through whom he acts.

Jesus is guiding us to a corporate reality he has prayed that the Father will bring to pass: that we as Witnesses of Union and Love will become one in heart and mind—a truly unified Community of Union and Love. We learn how to love with our brothers and sisters in Christ on the training field of relationships. By the Spirit of God at work among us, as the body of Christ, we are becoming one—just as Jesus and the Father are one (John 17:22–23).

We continue on our journey together in the School of Union and Love with Jesus. Next, we will draw on the Gospel of John and the other Gospels as we explore more of what it means to mature in love in Christ (1 Cor. 13:8–12). From there we will move into the New Testament, deeper into the letters of Paul, to discover what being "in Christ" means for you and me—and for the world God loves (John 3:16).

THE PRAYER

Lord Jesus, I am in you and you are in me. I thank you for the unfolding story of union and love in my own life. I welcome you to make me the kind of person who is a carrier of your wide, long, high, and deep love into all my relationships. In Christ Jesus, I pray, amen.

THE QUESTIONS

- What have you learned so far in our series about being in union with Jesus?

- What have you learned so far that has given you a renewed perspective on God's love for you and for others?

19

FOR GOD SO LOVED HE GAVE

JOHN 3:16–17

"For God so loved the world that he gave his one and only Son, that whoever believes in him shall not perish but have eternal life. For God did not send his Son into the world to condemn the world, but to save the world through him."

CONSIDER THIS

I knew her from the free breakfasts we would make for those living in the streets of our city. Friends would come from all over for those weekly morning meals, and we built community together as we swapped stories over pancakes and eggs.

One particular older woman, about the age of a grandmother, was an outcast among the others who came to the meal. She often smelled strongly of alcohol and body odor. Few would sit by her, not only because of the smell but also because she was brash and harsh with her words.

One day I was walking up the hill of the main street in our city, a few blocks away from our church offices. I had a lunch meeting with a friend that I was looking forward to. As I glanced up the street, however, there she was, right on my path. She was apparently arguing with someone who either wasn't there or who had walked away.

Something in me said, "Turn around; go another way." Then, someone in me—Christ in me—said, "Keep walking toward her." As I reached her I said, "Good morning!" and called her by name. She looked me up and down, then a scowl came over her face. "Give me money for coffee," she said. Not only did I not have cash on me at the time, but she wasn't being kind enough for me to want to help. I politely told her I had no money, and she scowled again as she barked, "You have money. You just don't want to give it to me." I apologized and kept going so I wouldn't be late for my meeting. Then, Christ in me spoke: "I love her. You have change in your desk drawer at the office. Go get it. Your meeting can wait."

I'd love to say my obedience was quick, but it wasn't. I argued with the Lord for at least a minute. I had someone else to honor, after all, and they would at least be nice to me. Then, I could feel something burning in my heart. It was the love of God for this precious daughter who had lost her way in life and found herself on the painful end of almost every relationship she ever had.

I turned and ran the few blocks to our offices. I actually hoped she wouldn't go away. I scraped up all the change I had in my drawer, then I ran back up the hill. She was still there. I smiled, catching my breath. "I have the money to buy you a coffee. Let's go." She paused, her eyes softening. "You went and got money for coffee?" I said yes. Then she leaned over and planted a motherly kiss on my cheek. She then squished my face between her hands, and said, "Thank you."

"For God so loved the world that he gave . . ."

I don't tell that story because I did something right, though I'm glad obedience won over my apathy, selfishness, and lack of attention to the voice of Jesus. I tell that story because God is a giver. And the quality of love we see in Jesus, the love of the Father incarnate, is the quality of love that dwells in you and me.

In Matthew 5:43–44, 46a, Jesus says: "You have heard that it was said, 'Love your neighbor and hate your enemy.' But I tell you, love your enemies and pray for those who persecute you . . . If you love those who love you, what reward will you get?"

Loving this woman in Jesus's name was hard for me. That is why he came to make his abode, his home, in us (John 14:23). His Spirit within us enables us to will and to do that which pleases the Father (Phil. 2:13).

Jesus gets us beyond ourselves.

Loving the world, in Jesus's name, is where the saving begins. Hearts become open to Jesus when they experience a love that surpasses what they had known before. Today, in the School of Union and Love, we learn that Jesus will help us love from within. He will help us do what we either won't do, or feel we cannot do.

God is a giver. By his grace, we are becoming givers too.

THE PRAYER

Lord Jesus, I am in you and you are in me. Forgive me when I have looked toward big opportunities to love others while leaving the small opportunities behind. Show me who you want me to love today in the world you love. I will obey. In Christ Jesus, I pray, amen.

THE QUESTIONS

- Have you had any experiences like the one in this story? If so, how willing were you to obey when the moment came and what did you learn about God's love for others?

20

APPRENTICES OF JESUS

JOHN 5:19

Jesus gave them this answer: "Very truly I tell you, the Son can do nothing by himself; he can do only what he sees his Father doing, because whatever the Father does the Son also does."

CONSIDER THIS

The year was 1488, and a man named Domenico Ghirlandaio was an Italian Renaissance painter in Italy. A young, thirteen-year-old boy became his apprentice, a boy who learned the art of fresco painting as part of his studies. Ghirlandaio had trained many apprentices, and all learned in a similar way—by watching and listening closely to him, paying attention to his direction and guidance, copying masterpieces to learn colors and strokes, and learning the ways of the trade.

Through focused observation and disciplined practice, they eventually learned their trade. His young thirteen-year-old apprentice, Michelangelo, certainly learned his trade well. He went on to paint the great frescoes of the Sistine Chapel. Then, with his further studies in the arts, he completed the dome of St. Peter's Cathedral, carved his famous *Pietà* and *David* statues from marble, and gave his elder, the great Leonardo da Vinci, a run for his money.

It all began with a good *apprenticeship*.

Jesus did what he saw the Father doing, and in so doing embodied the love the Creator has for humankind. Growing in union with Jesus, we are apprenticed to his way and the ways of the Father.

As Christians, we believe that Jesus took apprenticeship one giant step further than any master before or since. Jesus taught us his ways as our true Master, modeling them and inviting us, through practice, to learn how to love people in his name. Then, and here is the amazing part, he also made his home *in* us—leading our apprenticeship by his Spirit within! Now *that's* how to learn a master's ways.

In my ministry training in the Vineyard stream of churches, we were taught to ask one question with great frequency: "What is the Father doing?" Asking that question still remains part of my regular practice when I am asked to pray for someone or bring a word of encouragement.

Asking this question is intended to help us discern God's direction, to hear God's voice, about how the Father might be wanting to love that person in that particular moment. I know dozens of stories of moments when friends naturally wanted to pray one way for a person, but after asking the question, went another direction with their prayers. God did something powerful as a result, and they learned and grew from the experience. With practice, we can become better and better at discerning what the Father is doing.

"Anyone who has seen me has seen the Father" Jesus said in John 14:9b. We learn the Father's ways by watching Jesus, and listening to his voice. "My sheep listen to my voice; I know them, and they follow me" (John 10:27).

Being in union with Jesus as he lives within us and speaks by the Holy Spirit, we can learn to hear God's voice through constant practice and obedience.

Apprentices of Jesus learn from him by focused observation and disciplined practice. We learn by becoming attentive to his teaching in the Gospels and through the Scriptures, watching and learning from others who are practicing his way as well.

Doing what we see and sense the Father doing, we become like Jesus. Discipleship is a lifelong process of entering into an apprenticeship with Jesus until we become adept at doing what he does—thinking like he thinks, feeling like he feels, and acting like he acts. His presence within us makes this possible.

Today, you are invited to become an apprentice of Jesus.

THE PRAYER

Lord Jesus, I am in you and you are in me. I want to be your apprentice, guided and instructed by your Spirit within me. Teach me to ask what you are doing in every situation, and guide me as I grow in hearing and responding to your voice. In Christ Jesus, I pray, amen.

THE QUESTIONS

- Have you ever had a situation where you believe God spoke to you to do something different than your natural impulse? How did God speak to you, and what happened?

21

A NEW COMMAND

JOHN 13:34–35

"A new command I give you: Love one another. As I have loved you, so you must love one another. By this everyone will know that you are my disciples, if you love one another."

CONSIDER THIS

In many traditions of the church, one particular practice stands out as a compelling, visual illustration of the quality of love that Jesus intends to exist between him and his followers as well as among his followers. It is a practice that provides us with a metaphor for how we are to love one another as the world watches on.

Permit me to leave us in suspense for a bit for the sake of effect. This special practice was implemented by the early church (often before a Eucharist) and continues to be used by Methodists, Wesleyans, Anglicans, Lutherans, Mennonites, Presbyterians, Catholics, Orthodox

Christians, Pentecostals, Charismatics, and nondenominational Christians, by the Pope on Maundy Thursday, and by followers of Christ across cultures and millennia. It is a practice that is used as the central metaphor in viral social media posts encouraging us to love our enemies and in commercials reducing people to tears during the Super Bowl.

It is a practice that finds its roots in what Jesus did just before he spoke the words of John 13:34–35.

In John 13:1–17, just before his betrayal, Jesus gives his disciples a visual demonstration that is called the *Pedilavium* in some traditions. In some worship settings, a musical version of John 13:34 is sung as groups perform the ritual act to commemorate what Jesus did.

We're ready now to pull back the curtain. What did Jesus do that so many have memorialized?

Jesus poured water into a basin and began to *wash his disciples' feet.*

Knowing it was soon his time to go, knowing what would follow, and knowing that all power had been put in his hands, Jesus got up from the evening meal, took off his outer clothing, and put a towel around his waist.

It was a common practice in the ancient world to provide water for a sandaled guest to wash their own dusty feet when they entered a home. In some cases, a servant would wash the feet, or even the host of the gathering might wash the feet of the guest as well.

Jesus was showing them, physically demonstrating, that love humbles oneself, lowers oneself, to tenderly serve the other—regardless of either person's status or position in society.

God washes feet.

Peter is caught off guard that Jesus would do this and initially refuses. Then Jesus tells him, "Unless I wash you, you have no part with me" (v. 8). Peter then relents, and suggests Jesus wash his hands and head as well! Peter wants to completely "have part with" his Lord.

It's worth our time to read the next part together:

When he had finished washing their feet, he put on his clothes and returned to his place. "Do you understand what I have done for you?" he asked them. "You call me 'Teacher' and 'Lord,' and rightly so, for that is what I am. Now that I, your Lord and Teacher, have washed your feet, you also should wash one another's feet. I have set you an example that you should do as I have done for you. Very truly I tell you, no servant is greater than his master, nor is a messenger greater than the one who sent him. Now that you know these things, you will be blessed if you do them." (John 13:12–17)

This is the quality of love that Jesus is speaking of when he says in verses 34–35, "A new command I give you: Love one another. As I have loved you, so you must love one another. By this everyone will know that you are my disciples, if you love one another."

The word for love used here is *agape.* It is unconditional, valuing, esteeming, generous *love.*

If we, like Peter, want to have a part in Jesus, to be in union with Jesus, if we want the reality of his habitation in us and our habitation in him to take on its full meaning in the way we love one another, then we must allow Jesus to wash our feet. He washes our feet with his love and he meets us in our points of need as we come in humble and complete surrender. And, then, learning as apprentices, we are to take the next step in allowing him to wash the feet of others *through* us. We may do this physically as many church traditions do, or metaphorically as we act in humble love toward all we meet.

But either way, washing feet is the image behind the new command of Jesus—to love one another as he has loved us.

Jesus in us, and through us, is tying a cloth around his waist and getting ready to wash feet every single day. According to John 13:34–35, the world will not be won by people who spend most of their energy keeping to themselves, checking in on their investments from time to time, honing their religious practices to perfection, or even singing songs of faith with exuberance.

The world will be won by Jesus loving others through those who have learned to love one another like this—those who have actually become love in the process of washing feet.

In union with Jesus, we can wash feet—we can love one another in this way.

THE PRAYER

Lord Jesus, I am in you and you are in me. There are many feet to be washed in my circles of relationship. Show me whose feet I can wash with your love today. In Christ Jesus, I pray, amen.

THE QUESTIONS

- What opportunities have you had lately to humbly love and serve others?

- How has this new command of Jesus shown itself to bring more freedom to your life?

22

IF YOU KNOW, YOU KNOW

JOHN 14:6–7

Jesus answered, "I am the way and the truth and the life. No one comes to the Father except through me. If you really know me, you will know my Father as well. From now on, you do know him and have seen him."

CONSIDER THIS

I play a little game with my adult children. When I see a new internet acronym (acronyms like LOL, meaning "laugh out loud," or IMHO, meaning "in my humble opinion"), I attempt to guess what it means. If I can't figure it out immediately, I make things up that I think are funnier than the original. They cringe at my sense of humor, but I know deep down they think I should have my own stand-up comedy act. However, occasionally, I'm stumped.

A few years ago, this happened with IYKYK. If you don't already know what it means, IYKYK stands for "If you know, you know." In context, it is used to express that if you understand the image you are looking at, then you are part of a special crowd of people who have the unique background to understand that image (i.e., "If you know, you know"). The inference is that if you don't know what the image means, you're not part of their little in-crowd at that moment.

Jesus has his own version of IYKYK, but it means something very different. It is captured in John 14:6–7.

In today's passage, Jesus begins by declaring that he is the only Way, the only Truth, and the only Life given to humankind. He is the Way we know the Father, the Truth that guides us to the Father, and the Life that is found in the Father.

It is a radical statement, and it is why Christians were called followers of "the Way" in the earliest days (see Acts 9). He says that he is the Way to know the Father— and there is no other Way. Then Jesus follows this up with his version of an IYKYK statement: "If you really know me, you will know my Father as well. From now on, you do know him and have seen him" (v. 7).

He is saying, "If you *know* me, you *know* the Father." IYKYK.

When someone asks you to describe your version of God to them, how many of us fumble to say the right thing, hoping we don't blow the opportunity? What if we immediately began to describe all the qualities of Jesus? As the "radiance of God's glory and the exact representation of his being" (Heb. 1:3a), if you describe the character traits of Jesus, you describe the Father.

I was once asked to describe my version of God by a man I had just met. Thankfully, I described the qualities of Jesus. At the end of the conversation, he told me he couldn't deny that he liked the sound of that God. When I told him I was describing Jesus, and then explained the Trinity, he smiled and said he would rethink his thoughts about God.

IYKYK. If you know Jesus, you know the Father.

Now, what if people in your sphere of relationships began to text this acronym to one another: IYK [insert the first initial of your name] YKJ (i.e., If you know [insert your name], you know Jesus)? It may seem a bit beyond us right now, but according to 1 John 4:17, we are like him in this world.

With Jesus in you, the Father and all his love is in you. They have made their habitation in you (John 14:23). May people think of you when they think of Jesus. And when they think of Jesus in you, may they think that maybe they are beginning to see "all the fullness" (Eph. 3:19) of what God must be like.

THE PRAYER

Lord Jesus, I am in you and you are in me. I want to know you as I am known by you. I want to know the Father as I am known by the Father. I want to know the Spirit as I am known by the Spirit. Let people who know me, Jesus, see you in me today. In Christ Jesus, I pray, amen.

THE QUESTIONS

- Could you imagine your life becoming a reflection of the life of Jesus to this degree? What would it mean for you to allow his presence to shine through you ever more brightly as you age and mature in faith?

- How can you nurture that future, where people who meet you feel as though they have met Jesus?

23

THE LETTERS OF UNION AND LOVE

2 THESSALONIANS 3:17–18

I, Paul, write this greeting in my own hand, which is the distinguishing mark in all my letters. This is how I write. The grace of our Lord Jesus Christ be with you all.

CONSIDER THIS

Some of the most beautiful writing in history comes to us in the form of *letters*. Letters are personal, often written from the heart, and bear the thoughts, emotions, and character of the person writing.

Letters in the Bible can have a similar quality. God uses people, and when God gifts us with the written Word of God, he does so by having real people write the words (inspired by the Holy Spirit) that he wants delivered to us.

We now turn toward the letters of the Apostle of Union and Love, Paul.

Paul wrote many of the letters in the New Testament, sourced from his revelation of Jesus and fueled by his own deep, pastoral love for the people of God. Ephesians 3:14–21, a prayer written by Paul in a letter from prison to his brothers and sisters in Christ, carries the inspiration of the Holy Spirit moving through the prayer life of the apostle.

All of Paul's letters bear his tone, his wisdom, and his keen prophetic and prayerful instinct. They are also shaped by his deep knowledge of the Hebrew Scriptures, his love for the body of Christ, and his personal joys and sorrows.

In addition to speaking to us through the written Word, Jesus, dwelling in us, is speaking to the world today through your life and mine.

Some have said that your life may be the only letter from God that a person ever reads. Paul wrote that we are "God's handiwork, created in Christ Jesus to do good works, which God prepared in advance for us to do" (Eph. 2:10). The word for "handiwork" here is the Greek word *poiēma*, from where we get the word *poem*. You are God's poem to the world. And it is a beautiful poem he is writing.

May the poem of your life convey that every human heart, no matter how distant from God one may feel, can come into loving union with God through Christ.

And the themes of union and love permeate the letters of Paul. They flow from the inspiration of the Holy

Spirit, rushing like a river through Paul's voice. When he writes with such passion about us being "in Christ," a phrase (with its variations) appearing with great frequency in his letters, he is writing about all we have just learned from Jesus in the Gospel of John.

Paul wants us to know, needs us to know, that we are abiding in Christ (John 15:4–5), united to Christ (17:23), in all things. Paul wants us to know—needs us to know—that *nothing* will ever separate us from Christ's love.

Passages from Paul's letters we are about to explore speak of Jesus a) living in us as his *habitation*; b) inviting us to *participation* in his life, death, and resurrection; and c) transforming us to become an *incarnation* of his loving presence in the world.

When Paul writes about us being the *habitation* of Jesus, he is communicating that we are individually and corporately a temple in which the Spirit of the Living God lives (1 Cor. 6:19–20). When he writes about sharing in the life of Jesus in full *participation*, he is communicating that we are identified with Jesus in his life, death, and resurrection (Phil. 3:10–11). And when Paul writes about us becoming an *incarnation* of the love of Jesus to the world, he is communicating that we can come to a place where it is no longer you or I who live—but Christ who lives in us (Gal. 2:20).

Paul is a man who was changed by union and love. His words about our identification with Jesus and Jesus's

  DAN WILT

identification with us and his church have shaped the theology of the body of Christ for thousands of years. For Paul, that union uniquely hosts the possibility that our lives will bear the fruit of holy love—a Jesus-quality of love that continues to confound the loves of this world.

As the Apostle of Union and Love, Paul's letters will help us understand the benefits, the challenges, and the glory of being united with Christ.

THE PRAYER

Lord Jesus, I am in you and you are in me. As your poem to the world, use me to do good works in your name. You have artfully crafted my life with love, and I want my life to carry the theme that you, Jesus, truly save. In Christ Jesus, I pray, amen.

THE QUESTIONS

- Have you ever thought of your life as a poem to the world, written by God in the ink of love?

- Do you have a favorite passage from one of Paul's letters that continues to help you on your journey of knowing Jesus?

INSEPARABLE

ROMANS 5:5; 8:35, 38–39

And hope does not put us to shame, because God's love has been poured out into our hearts through the Holy Spirit, who has been given to us.

Who shall separate us from the love of Christ? Shall trouble or hardship or persecution or famine or nakedness or danger or sword? . . . For I am convinced that neither death nor life, neither angels nor demons, neither the present nor the future, nor any powers, neither height nor depth, nor anything else in all creation, will be able to separate us from the love of God that is in Christ Jesus our Lord.

CONSIDER THIS

Many years ago, I was with my family on a beautiful sailboat owned and piloted by dear friends. Out in the middle of Lake Ontario on a warm day, my oldest daughter and I decided to get in the calm water as the boat floated quietly beside us. She was thirteen at the time, and we both had on life preservers. We swam right beside the boat, adjusting to the cold water and thinking we might get out sooner than we had thought.

Then, the wind suddenly grew strong and the water became choppy. Before we could even turn toward the boat, a gust whisked it away rapidly until it was some distance from us. I turned to see that my daughter was still a few feet away from me. Before I could get to her, a large swell began to separate us.

I could see the fear rising in her eyes. With all my strength and a father's inner resolve (if you're a dad, you know exactly what I mean), I was going to get to her *no matter what.* I swam in a direct line to her as fast as I could as the waves pushed me back. Finally, I reached her. We grasped hands firmly and I drew her close. We turned toward the boat, and I saw my skillful, sailing friend cutting through the wind—pulling up right beside us like a chauffeur for our ride home.

What had threatened to separate us was no match for my resolve and my friend's skill. In my father's heart, separation was simply *not an option.*

In this famous passage on love, Paul is declaring that God's love will not allow a separation to happen when a heart is reaching toward him. Separation is not an option for Jesus. Our union is at the center of his attention and focus. Yet, facing trouble, hardship, persecution, famine, nakedness, danger, sword, death, life, angels, demons, present, future, height, depth, can make it *seem* as though we have been left to ourselves in a cold, hard world.

But Paul has a point to make, a point with which we as modern Christians must come to grips. He is saying that our union with Jesus is an *unbreakable* bond. When suffering or difficulty comes, as followers of Jesus, we should always assume that God is with us in that suffering.

Let that sink in. I'll repeat it. When suffering or difficulty comes, we should always assume that God is with us in that suffering. We are in union with him. He loves us. We are *inseparable*.

Our faith in God's love for us must be more powerful—more resilient, more unshakeable, more real—than our faith in our circumstances.

St. John of the Cross, writing in his famous *Dark Night of the Soul,* suggested that suffering will come to us, and we will be changed when it does. As suffering comes, he believed it could deliver us from old habits of the heart into a deeper experience of union with God in Christ.

Just as I did with my daughter that day on the lake, Jesus closes gaps that threaten to separate us. He does so by the power of his love for us. The reality of suffering does not mean Jesus does not love you. Suffering means that you have another opportunity to turn toward him, to depend on him, and to learn what true love is all about.

His love will always come after you.

THE PRAYER

Lord Jesus, I am in you and you are in me. I often interpret gaps in my sense of feeling blessed or cared for as gaps in your love for me. Deliver me from believing that suffering is an indication of your disappointment; help me to see that suffering can be a path to deeper intimacy with you. In Christ Jesus, I pray, amen.

THE QUESTIONS

- Have you interpreted suffering or difficulty as a lack of God's affection or attention in your life? What would happen if you began to see suffering as an opportunity to grow closer to Jesus?

UNITED WITH THE RESURRECTED JESUS

ROMANS 6:4–8

We were therefore buried with him through baptism into death in order that, just as Christ was raised from the dead through the glory of the Father, we too may live a new life.

For if we have been united with him in a death like his, we will certainly also be united with him in a resurrection like his. For we know that our old self was crucified with him so that the body ruled by sin might be done away with, that we should no longer be slaves to sin—because anyone who has died has been set free from sin.

Now if we died with Christ, we believe that we will also live with him.

CONSIDER THIS

United.

It's a powerful word. To be united with others speaks of being connected to those people. We may share values, dreams, hopes, and actions—moving in one accord with another. We may share ideas, aspirations, intentions, and goals—moving as one toward their fulfillment.

When the term *united* is applied to states, it means those states are connected by shared resources, government structure, a flag, a vision of a preferred future, and national aspirations for the health and well-being of citizens. When the term *united* is applied to soccer teams, it means that people are connected by shared mascots, logos, chants, uniforms, love for the game, thrilling victories, agonizing defeats, and aspirations for a championship season.

But when *united* is applied between two people who love one another, unity takes on a deeper layer of meaning. We move as one with that person. We are connected, joined, bonded, often in unspoken ways. In more intimate relationships, we may begin to feel inseparable from that person, even joined at the heart. In close friendships, we may feel seen and known by the other, laughing at the same jokes or finishing one another's sentences.

In Romans 6:4–8, a true Easter passage, Paul tells us we are *united* with Christ.

The Greek word used here for "united," *symphytos*, speaks of two things that have been planted and have grown together. In other words, they are *intertwined*.

According to Paul, our lives are intertwined with Jesus. We move as one with him. We are bonded in unspoken ways. We are inseparable from him. We are joined at the heart. I personally aspire to laugh at the same jokes and finish his sentences!

Paul goes even further than this. United with Jesus, we identify with him in his death, and we participate with him in his resurrection life. Intertwined with him, our old self of sin died with him and was buried. Intertwined with him, our new-creation self was raised with him and participates in the fullness of his life at every moment.

The sacramental image of baptism—a profound Easter image that expresses the heart of Romans 6:4—says more than words can say. Baptism is the immersion of a believer in water, a sacred enactment of us dying in union with the suffering Christ (going under) and rising in union with the resurrected Christ (coming up).

And this participation in Christ's death and resurrection is *real*, made possible by the Holy Spirit. You are no longer dead in your sin! You are alive to God in Christ (Rom. 6:11)! Baptism is more than a symbol—it is a sacramental sign of a new reality unfolding in the life of the believer.

With our lives united with the resurrected Jesus, we are invited to be full participants in the timeless love story between God and his people.

We are united with Christ.

THE PRAYER

Lord Jesus, I am in you and you are in me. To know that my old self no longer rules over me is cause for worship. I died with you, never to be enslaved by sin again. I am raised with you, alive to righteousness, peace, and joy in the Holy Spirit (Rom. 14:17). I choose to live, united with you, my Lord. In Christ Jesus, I pray, amen.

THE QUESTIONS

- What does it mean to you to be united with Jesus in his death and resurrection?

- What is the story of your baptism?

- Do you have stories highlighting how you were raised to new life in Christ?

26

IN CHRIST WE ARE FREE

ROMANS 8:1–4

Therefore, there is now no condemnation for those who are in Christ Jesus, because through Christ Jesus the law of the Spirit who gives life has set you free from the law of sin and death. For what the law was powerless to do because it was weakened by the flesh, God did by sending his own Son in the likeness of sinful flesh to be a sin offering. And so he condemned sin in the flesh, in order that the righteous requirement of the law might be fully met in us, who do not live according to the flesh but according to the Spirit.

CONSIDER THIS

There is a phrase from old Westerns that has become well-used over the years. It has become an idiom used by comedians, athletes, politicians, and actors. The phrase has come to mean, "The old way of doing things is out. A new way of doing things—*my way*—is in."

That phrase is: "There's a new sheriff in town."

In today's verse, Paul tells the Romans, "There's a new *law* in town." The law of sin and death has lost its seat of influence in your life and mine. The law of the Spirit, who gives life, has set us free. There's a new boss in town, and that means we can tell the old bosses—sin and death—to take a hike whenever either tries to claim authority.

To mix metaphors, for those who are "in Christ," the law of sin and death is no longer in the driver's seat. The law of sin and death no longer has mastery over us. Jesus remedied that. We don't answer to sin, defer to death, or remain chained to our old ways of thinking, feeling, or acting like lost people. We don't wallow in self-condemnation or act as though Christ has done nothing to set us free from old, broken patterns.

If we do, we are not living from our union with Christ. We may need help to get free from old ways that lead to sin and death, yes, but the truth that empowers our transformation in Christ is the foundation for our healing: in Christ, you are *free*.

My brothers and sisters, today we have been invited to live within the broad and sweeping, powerful and freeing law of the Spirit! And it's an invitation to which we must say yes if we want to experience the abundant life Jesus promised.

We are intertwined, heart and soul aligned—with Jesus. Christ became a sin-offering for us, reconciling us to God and giving us the ministry of reconciliation (2 Cor. 5:18–19). For freedom, you and I have been set free, no longer (with Christ in you and you in Christ) to be subject to that nasty yoke of sin-slavery ever again (Gal. 5:1).

Abiding in Jesus, we live and move in the law of the Spirit. And the Spirit gives life! Imagine the words of the Nicene Creed being shouted from a rooftop: *"We believe in the Holy Spirit, the Lord, the giver of life!"*

Jesus sets us free to enjoy life. In the Spirit! He who knew no sin became sin for us that we might become right-related to God, ourselves, others, and the creation (2 Cor. 5:21). His right-heartedness is our right-heartedness.

Welcome to the Spirit-filled, Spirit-healed, Spirit-renewed family of God.

Our daily work as believers is to remember, reclaim, and rehearse the benefits that come from living in the freedom of the Spirit. We live in the "new way of the Spirit" (Rom. 7:5–6).

If you are in union with Christ, you are a recipient of all his benefits (Ps. 103:2–5). One of those benefits is that right now, at this very moment, you live within the roomy and healing realm of the Spirit. If the Son sets you free, you are "free indeed" (John 8:36), and "where the Spirit of the Lord is, there is freedom" (2 Cor. 3:17).

There's a new law in town—the law of the Spirit of life. And it sets captives *free*.

THE PRAYER

Lord Jesus, I am in you and you are in me. I want to live in the freedom of the law of the Spirit. When I forget my inheritance and am tempted to sin to ease my pain, I am grateful for forgiveness and the continued call to the freedom I have in you. In Christ Jesus, I pray, amen.

THE QUESTIONS

- How have you lived out the "I'm worthy of condemnation" message in your life? Has it kept you chained to guilt for your sins, even the ones for which Jesus has forgiven you, rather than setting you free to live a Spirit-filled life?

27

IN CHRIST WE ARE ONE BODY

ROMANS 12:5, 10

So in Christ we, though many, form one body, and each member belongs to all the others. . . . Be devoted to one another in love. Honor one another above yourselves.

CONSIDER THIS

As our children were growing up, we had a saying in our home: "Friends will come and go, but family is forever." When a minor scrap would break out between siblings (as one sometimes did), or friendships would get in the way of sibling relationships (as they sometimes did), we would come back to this principle time and time again.

We also worked hard to guide our children never to speak ill of their siblings. "Words create worlds," it's been said, and we wanted them to create a good story in their own minds, and in the minds of their siblings, about their most precious and lasting relationships. After all, we are *family*. We have now had the privilege of watching a beautiful reality play out—our grown children love one another deeply.

I often think about the phrase "family is forever" when I read today's passage from Romans 12:5. Paul is resonating with the teaching of Jesus in John 17:20–23 about the family of God and the purity of our relationships with one another. In a very real way, family members *belong* to one another. We are like one body caring for itself. Our actions impact the others in our circle of love, and real care should be taken to serve one another given our integration with the lives of the others.

Paul, seeing Christ as the head of the body—a metaphor he found quite useful—affirmed Jesus as the leader of our family (Eph. 4:15). Just as my children are in me as their father, and I am in them as my children, in a similar way we as the church are in Christ—and he is in us.

And that is where union with Christ meets real-world application. The bond of love between family members has primacy in all our relational interactions. As a friend once put it, "We fight for love."

Therefore, if my sister or brother is in pain, then I am in pain. We fight for love.

It's a family thing.

If a family member of another political perspective or ethnic background is in pain, then I am in pain. We fight for love.

It's a family thing.

It is only in this identifying with, and honoring of, our family members that real healing can occur in churches or society. Family is the paradigm that will bring the healing in the body of Christ that we all desire.

I simply cannot allow my disagreement with a family member to compromise my love for them or stop me from taking actions that serve and honor them even in the midst of disagreement or misalignment. We can be truthful and loving at the same time. In fact, we must. We are in Christ, together.

It's a family thing.

Here we must take a deep breath and, quite honestly, grow up in Christ. It's not easy, but it's necessary. Jesus in you, and Jesus in me, means we do not abruptly leave those with whom we disagree without pursuing reconciliation (though we are honest in the process). Jesus in you, and Jesus in me, means we do not talk behind backs, dehumanize people in response to a newscast or social media post, or laugh when someone falls hard.

We belong to Jesus, and we belong to one another. Union with Christ reminds us of this irrepressible truth. Family love can be costly, but it is the welcome cost that comes with union with Christ and union with his people.

Jesus prayed that "all of them [us] may be one, Father, just as you are in me and I am in you. May they also be in us so that the world may believe that you have sent me"

　　　　DAN WILT

(John 17:21). Belonging to one another, and living out that membership in one another, is the primary evidence that we are actually in union with Jesus as a community.

Come, Lord Jesus. Help us be one.

Paul puts it this way later in his letter: "Be devoted to one another in love. Honor one another above yourselves" (Rom. 12:10). Putting our union with Christ and one another ahead of our most firmly held opinions, valuing being loving more than being right, we can become one.

Followers of Jesus are one family, in union with Christ. In this reality lie the seeds of our healing.

THE PRAYER

Lord Jesus, I am in you and you are in me. I recognize today that being in union with you means being in union with those who are in the covenant family of God. I resist the impulse to place my opinions before my love, to place my views before my care. In Christ Jesus, I pray, amen.

THE QUESTIONS

- Have you ever experienced belonging to another brother or sister who didn't share your personal views? If so, what was that like and how has it impacted you?

IN CHRIST WE ARE SANCTIFIED

1 CORINTHIANS1:2–3

To the church of God in Corinth, to those sanctified in Christ Jesus and called to be his holy people, together with all those everywhere who call on the name of our Lord Jesus Christ—their Lord and ours: Grace and peace to you from God our Father and the Lord Jesus Christ.

CONSIDER THIS

To be "sanctified in Christ Jesus" means that Jesus has made us holy by his work on the cross. We are set apart and pure in the sight of God. We are seen through the lens of Christ. From that position of being made holy in the sight of God by the saving work of Jesus, the saints (which means "holy ones") are engaged in a transformative process of sanctification that touches every area of our lives. Let's talk about that process.

The process of ongoing sanctification, or ongoing transformation into Christlikeness, simply means that God is at work within us to make us like Jesus. In other words, we are sanctified before God because we are in Christ Jesus (Rom. 1:2) *and* because of this union, God is transforming our lives daily to become human as he intended.

Let me illustrate this idea of ongoing sanctification, which is rooted in being sanctified in Christ Jesus.

When I first met my friend, he was not a follower of Jesus. His demeanor was one of anger, confusion, and self-protection. He was a man who had a hard life, and his heart matched it. But . . . *God.*

God's grace had been drawing him his entire life. After some conversations between us, he decided to visit our church one morning. At the end of the message, I gave an invitation to come to the front to surrender to Jesus. He began to walk toward the front and many eyes in the room welled up with tears. We gathered around him in love, and as we prayed for him, he came to Jesus. He was sanctified, made holy, in Christ Jesus.

What happened next surprised me, in the best of ways. He was in Jesus. Jesus was in him. Weeks began to pass. He began to learn the way of Jesus. He was taught about his union with Jesus and about the love of the Father for him and others. He immersed himself in worship every time our doors were opened. His hands, raised high in worship week after week, were clean—right along with his heart (Ps. 24:4).

I watched the transformation with my own eyes; we all did. The Spirit was at work in him, conforming him to Jesus. He began to evidence the fruit of the Spirit in Galatians 5. He began to express love in a 1 Corinthians 13 manner. He started to become a peaceful presence in my own life and was generous with his love and care. Then, over months, he began to selflessly minister to others in remarkable ways. He was a *changed* man.

Grace had drawn him into union with Jesus. Grace had saved him through Jesus. Grace was now transforming him, from glory to glory, into the likeness of Christ. And all along the way, his eyes were softened by the love of God for him.

"And we all, who with unveiled faces contemplate the Lord's glory, are being transformed into his image with ever-increasing glory, which comes from the Lord, who is the Spirit" (2 Cor. 3:18).

Sanctification means we are set apart as God's people and the Spirit within us is making us like Jesus as our lives are offered to him in completeness. The Spirit of Jesus is at work in us, loving us, living through us, changing us—from glory to glory. We begin to practice the way of Jesus in all aspects of our lives, public and private, and the Spirit changes our attitudes, our motives, our affections, and our desires.

We nurture communion with him, and we begin to desire an awareness of his presence more than anything else. We fix our eyes on him, we go through trials that test our faith, and we run the race set before us (Heb. 12:1–3).

Sanctification means that Jesus, living in you and you in him, is taking over. You are on a journey to become like him, changed by his relentless love for you. As an apprentice trains to become like his or her master, you are in training (1 Cor. 9:25–27). You will not find comfort or rest in remaining as you are, nor in behaving in ways that are more like your family upbringing than they are like Jesus. Your attitude is on its way to becoming the same attitude of Jesus, who took on the nature of a servant (Phil. 2:5–11).

Like a caterpillar turning into a butterfly, you may not always love the process, but you will love the result. You will bear the good fruit of love, joy, peace, patience, kindness, goodness, faithfulness, gentleness, and self-control (Gal. 5:22–23). He is faithful, and he will do it (1 Thess. 5:24)!

Here is the best part. His heart will grow within you. Your eyes will shine with the light of Jesus, like sanctuary lights radiating through stained glass on a winter's night.

Sanctification is about Jesus making you a sanctuary of his presence, lighting the world with the love that is lighting you. We are made holy, sanctified, perfected in God's life and love, by our covenant union with Jesus. Then, we are daily transformed in Christlikeness. He is in you, at work in you, to accomplish the goal of you coming into the "measure of all the fullness of God" (Eph. 3:19).

THE PRAYER

Lord Jesus, I am in you and you are in me. Let your sanctifying work continue in me. Transform my thoughts, words, actions, and the inner attitudes of my heart into your own. In Christ Jesus, I pray, amen.

THE QUESTIONS

- Have you ever heard the word *sanctification* before? If so, what did you think it meant?

- How has your understanding changed as you read today's entry?

29

IN CHRIST WE HAVE A NEW WAY OF LIFE

1 CORINTHIANS 4:16–17

Therefore I urge you to imitate me. For this reason I have sent to you Timothy, my son whom I love, who is faithful in the Lord. He will remind you of my way of life in Christ Jesus, which agrees with what I teach everywhere in every church.

CONSIDER THIS

Habits are all the rage right now. The book *Atomic Habits* by James Clear is one of the bestsellers of our day. Social media is full of habit talk—how to break bad habits, how to start good habits, and how to create habits that help you achieve your goals in life.

Have you ever tried to build a good habit or break a bad one? It's not easy to learn a new way of doing daily life, especially as we age. But what if the Spirit of the eternal God is living in you, transforming your habits to make you like Jesus? That is a different story.

Our habits add up to our *way of life*, and if our habits are on point with Jesus, then our way of life will slowly—increasingly—make us like Jesus (1 John 4:17). We'll embody the virtues of Jesus, evidencing the fruit of the Spirit as we learn to act with love, joy, peace, patience, kindness, goodness, faithfulness, gentleness, and self-control (Gal. 5:22–23). When Paul tells the Corinthians that Timothy will remind them of his way of life (1 Cor. 4:16–17), I believe that Timothy was not only reminding them with words. Timothy was also an example of the way of life of Jesus. He most probably even imitated Paul (v. 16) on his journey to being like Christ.

The earliest followers of Jesus were called followers of "the Way." The term could be understood to have different meanings. Jesus called himself the "way and the truth and the life" in John 14:6. "No one comes to the Father" except through him, the way to God.

But Jesus also had a way of life he taught his disciples. They were his apprentices. Before we came to faith in Jesus, we had a former way of life (Gal. 1:14; Eph. 4:22), and now, by grace, we have a new way of life in Christ (1 Cor. 4:17).

This is the point Paul is making in 1 Corinthians 4:17. Timothy is going to remind the Corinthians of Paul's

 DAN WILT

"way of life *in Christ Jesus*." In other words, Paul is living a life of love (Eph. 5:2) in union with Jesus. In fact, Paul will go so far as to say that Jesus is living his life through him (Gal. 2:20). Paul could confidently say that his habits and way of being in the world were to be imitated as he imitated Christ (1 Cor. 4:16; 11:1).

In the first few centuries of the church, Christians would be thoroughly discipled to become like Jesus in thought, word, and action. They would be coached, often by mentors, on how to grow in their spiritual union with Jesus. These early believers went into deep training (1 Cor. 9:24–25) to transform how they responded to their experiences in the pagan world with their thoughts, emotions, and bodies. They had to deeply learn a new way of life—to become different people—or they were destined to fall back into their old ways:

> You were taught, with regard to your former way of life, to put off your old self, which is being corrupted by its deceitful desires; to be made new in the attitude of your minds; and to put on the new self, created to be like God in true righteousness and holiness.
>
> Therefore each of you must put off falsehood and speak truthfully to your neighbor . . . (Eph. 4:22–25a)

Like us, they had much to unlearn as they learned their new way of life. Their training was a partnership with the indwelling Spirit's transformation of their heart. By learning new habits such as meeting frequently with other believers; worshipping; praying; visiting the poor, the sick, and the imprisoned, maintaining purity; acting truthfully, and much more, they were slowly and thoroughly converted from their pagan ways to a Christlike way of responding to the world.[9]

As we practice the way of Jesus, we begin to grow in our desire to be like the one who loves us more than we could imagine. And as we grow in that desire and practice habits of the heart that shape our way of life, Jesus aligns our way of life with his own.

THE PRAYER

Lord Jesus, I am in you and you are in me. Transform me in my inner self, habit of the heart by habit of the heart, until I become like you in every way. Let my way of life be a sign to all those I meet that you live in your people. In Christ Jesus, I pray, amen.

---

9. For a helpful list of early church discipleship habits, see Alan Kreider, *The Patient Ferment of the Early Church: The Improbable Rise of Christianity in the Roman Empire* (Grand Rapids: Baker Academic, 2016), 122–23.

THE QUESTIONS

- Is the Lord teaching you new habits of the heart? What are they?

- Do you feel the Spirit's help as you progress toward becoming like him?

30

IN CHRIST OUR BODIES ARE THE TEMPLE OF THE SPIRIT

1 CORINTHIANS 6:15, 17, 19–20

Do you not know that your bodies are members of Christ himself? Shall I then take the members of Christ and unite them with a prostitute? Never! . . . But whoever is united with the Lord is one with him in spirit. . . .

Do you not know that your bodies are temples of the Holy Spirit, who is in you, whom you have received from God? You are not your own; you were bought at a price. Therefore honor God with your bodies.

CONSIDER THIS

If you are like me, you enjoy your independence. In charge of myself, I can do what I want, when I want. For those of us who live in the United States, that version of freedom is deeply ingrained within us as a culture.

When someone else is in charge of me, I bristle under their direction. I may even resist guidance and obedience. Even if love is behind that guidance, and following another's direction might be for my best, I may still press to do things my own way.

In today's passage, Paul is resolved, unflinching, in his address to a wayward group of Christians. He wants to communicate that each individual, and then all of them as a community, are in union with Jesus. To summarize Paul: "You belong to Christ, your spirit as well as your body. You are not your own."

You belong to Jesus.

This is an idea that is deeply rooted in the ancient covenant relationship God has with his people. As we read today's passages, one can hear the echoes of Isaiah's words in Isaiah 43:1: "But now, this is what the LORD says—he who created you, Jacob, he who formed you, Israel: 'Do not fear, for I have redeemed you; I have summoned you by name; you are mine.'" We are a people who belong to God, a royal priesthood in covenant relationship with our Creator (1 Peter 2:9).

Paul is communicating that we must understand our bodies as being in union with Jesus, belonging to Christ.

We are temples of the Holy Spirit (1 Cor. 6:19). He is teaching us that one step on the path to experiencing the "measure of all the fullness of God" and "to know this love that surpasses knowledge" (Eph. 3:19) is to steward and protect how we use our bodies, our holy temples, along this narrow way.

In a day when independence from God is seen as true liberation, Paul is trying to say that our union with Christ—belonging in whole to our master and savior—is freedom in its purest form. Our bodies are so precious to God that what we do with them is uniting Jesus with that action. Honoring Jesus with our body is paramount for growing in union with Christ.

Paul's vision of union with Jesus is powerful. He helps us understand why offering our bodies to God is so important to our discipleship (Rom. 12:1–2). Our bodies belong to Jesus—the one who most loves and cares for us.

THE PRAYER

Lord Jesus, I am in you and you are in me. I will honor you with my body, as I belong to you. I will use my body, the temple of your Holy Spirit, to honor you. I will give you glory through both my public and private actions, knowing you are always in me. In Christ Jesus, I pray, amen.

 DAN WILT

THE QUESTIONS

- There is a strong identification of Jesus with both his church and with its individual members. Do you feel that union with Christ daily in both private and public?

- How do you use your body to glorify God?

IN CHRIST WE LEARN THE WAY OF LOVE (PART ONE)

1 CORINTHIANS 13:4–13

Love is patient, love is kind. It does not envy, it does not boast, it is not proud. It does not dishonor others, it is not self-seeking, it is not easily angered, it keeps no record of wrongs. Love does not delight in evil but rejoices with the truth. It always protects, always trusts, always hopes, always perseveres.

Love never fails. But where there are prophecies, they will cease; where there are tongues, they will be stilled; where there is knowledge, it will pass away. For we know in part and we prophesy in part, but when completeness comes, what is in part disappears. When I was a child, I talked like a child, I thought like a child, I reasoned like a child. When I became a man, I put the ways of childhood behind me. For now we see only a reflection as in a mirror; then we shall see face to face. Now I know in part; then I shall know fully, even as I am fully known.

And now these three remain: faith, hope and love. But the greatest of these is love.

We can confidently say that 1 Corinthians 13:4–13 stands as one of the most profound articulations of love in world literature. Its verses have been quoted by presidents, read at weddings the world over, and have served as a guiding light for Christians learning to love like Jesus for thousands of years. Whatever may have happened to Paul on the road to Damascus in Acts 9, whatever he may have experienced as he learned the gospel by revelation from Jesus (Gal. 1:11–12), it found its way to the surface in this remarkable passage about the way of love.

Paul is expanding on the love of Christ he describes in his Prayer of Union and Love in Ephesians 3:14–21. For that reason, we will take the time to savor the verses from this passage over a few days. We will draw fresh insights into our union with Christ from this Spirit-inspired and instructive vision of love—a passage that teaches us how to love others as Jesus loves us (John 13:34).

As we begin, I would like to draw on writing about 1 Corinthians 13 by my good friend J. D. Walt. He provides an exercise in love that can begin to help us actualize and incorporate the love of Jesus into our thinking and actions.

I would welcome you to do the exercises he suggests along with me:

First Corinthians 13 is profound realism. As an exercise of faith and bold self-examination, I want to ask you to insert your name in every blank below. Read it aloud inserting your name in each blank.

> _______ is patient. _______ is kind. _______ does not envy, _______ does not boast, _______ is not proud. _______ does not dishonor others, _______ is not self-seeking, _______ is not easily angered, _______ keeps no record of wrongs. _______ does not delight in evil but rejoices with the truth. _______ always protects, _______ always trusts, _______ always hopes, _______ always perseveres.

"This is impossible!" you say. And you are right, if it is solely up to you and me to become these things. Here's the big secret.

Go back and insert the word "Jesus" in all the blanks. If these things are true about Jesus, and we know they are, and Jesus is in you, what does that say about you?[10]

We can learn Christ's way of love because Christ Jesus is in us. Of all the transforming passages in the

10. J. D. Walt, *What Happens in Corinth* (Franklin, TN: Seedbed Publishing, 2021), 154–55.

DAN WILT

Scriptures, these verses would be worth memorizing and rehearsing in the coming days.

In union with Jesus, we can learn the way of love.

THE PRAYER

Lord Jesus, I am in you and you are in me. The kind of love Paul describes here is only possible if you are living your life through me. My life's work is to allow you to do that. In union with you, I choose to align my spirit with the way of love as it is described here. "Teach me your way, Lord," that I may walk in your truth (Ps. 86:11). Teach me to love as you love. In Christ Jesus, I pray, amen.

THE QUESTIONS

- What do you think would happen if you did both exercises once per day for one month?

- What do you think might change in the way you experience God's love and in the way you love others?

IN CHRIST WE LEARN THE WAY OF LOVE (PART TWO)

1 CORINTHIANS 13:4

Love is patient, love is kind. It does not envy, it does not boast, it is not proud.

CONSIDER THIS

Have you ever considered the patience of Jesus? Knowing his story was leading to a cross, he still patiently served his disciples and ministered to those who came to him. We never perceive that Jesus was in a rush, or biding his time to get to something else.

Have you ever considered the kindness of Jesus? Continually asked to do things, be things . . . to make things happen, we see him responding with clarity and grace even in circumstances where the needs seem to be overwhelming.

Then we see Jesus moving in contentment; we don't hear envy or comparison with others in his words. Neither does he boast or exhibit arrogance.

With today's section of 1 Corinthians 13:4–13, let's repeat our exercise of inserting the name of Jesus in the place of love first, and then inserting our own names second as a declaration of our union with Jesus:

> *Love is patient, love is kind. It does not envy, it does not boast, it is not proud.*
>
> *Jesus is patient, Jesus is kind. Jesus does not envy, Jesus does not boast, Jesus is not proud.*
>
> *[Insert your name] is patient, [Insert your name] is kind. [Insert your name] does not envy, [insert your name] does not boast, [insert your name] is not proud.*

Because the Spirit of Jesus lives in you and me (Phil. 1:19; Gal. 4:6), *we can be patient.* When we say, "I am an impatient person," we are contradicting our union with Christ. We may be well-meaning and may have grown up believing that self-effacing comments are a sign of humility, but we are not agreeing with God when we make them. Christ in you is patient; therefore, he is transforming you into a patient person.

We can be kind. We can put a gentle hand toward the hearts of those who come across our path (in person, via text, or on social media). A feeling of outrage over what someone posts is no excuse for losing our cool and dehumanizing them with our language. "In your anger do not sin" (Eph. 4:26), we are told. Christ in you is kind; therefore, he is transforming you into a kind person.

We can avoid envy, boasting, and pride. Envy tells us the lie that someone has it better than us. Who has it better than a beloved child of God? No one has it better. Boasting is what we do when we are insecure and attempt to heighten our reputation in the presence of another. Who has a higher reputation than Christ in us, and what child of God is desperate for someone to affirm us when Jesus himself affirms us as his own? And as for pride, Paul will only boast in Jesus, and in his own weaknesses (1 Cor. 1:31; 2 Cor. 12:9). A beautiful humility is the consistent posture of Jesus's disciples in the world.

In union with Jesus, you and I can become the most loving people on planet Earth. We can do so not because we have it all together or because we have no weaknesses with which we struggle. We can become the most loving people on planet Earth because Jesus—the most loving person who ever lived and ever will—dwells in us.

THE PRAYER

Lord Jesus, I am in you and you are in me. There is a fear I have of waiting, and my union with you is conquering that fear in me even now as I pray. I want

     DAN WILT

to become patient, and by this union with you, I will. I want to become more kind, and by this union with you, I will. I want to leave envy, arrogance, and pride behind me, and by this union with you, I will. In Christ Jesus, I pray, amen.

THE QUESTIONS

- Do you see yourself as naturally patient, naturally kind, naturally content, naturally elevating of others, naturally humble? If you answered yes on any one of these, wonderful!

- What area is Christ in you working on right now to make you more mature in other areas?

IN CHRIST WE LEARN THE WAY OF LOVE (PART THREE)

1 CORINTHIANS 13:5

[Love] does not dishonor others, it is not self-seeking, it is not easily angered, it keeps no record of wrongs.

CONSIDER THIS

Isn't it fascinating how Jesus honors a humble heart in the Gospels? The story of Zacchaeus is a perfect example. His heart was turned toward Jesus, and Jesus responded by honoring him with a house visit (Luke 19:1–10). Jesus didn't have to put his reputation on the line to go to the home of a chief tax collector. But God gives grace to the humble (James 4:6).

Jesus is also the embodiment of selflessness. While we can imagine Jesus took care of his own basic needs, his selfless orientation of the heart is to see others lifted up, encouraged, and drawn to the Father. Jesus's lifestyle is the opposite of a "selfie" lifestyle; Christ's love seeks the good of the other.

In our anger, we don't have to sin (Eph. 4:26a). There are moments when Jesus seems to be expressing anger toward the highly religious who are misguiding the faithful. But from 2 Corinthians 5:21, we understand that Jesus was without sin in those moments. Any anger he did convey would have been truly righteous anger. However, even in those moments, we don't get the picture that Jesus was easily angered. He was quick to love and slow to anger.

Jesus is compassionate and gracious, abounding in love (Ps. 103:8). When a Pharisee became tender to the gospel, Jesus graciously gave them his time and teaching (John 3:21). We never perceive that Jesus is holding grudges or withholding grace from someone who is open to seeing the error of their ways.

With today's section of 1 Corinthians 13:4–13 in our hearts, let's repeat our exercise of inserting the name of Jesus in the place of love first and then inserting our own names second. We will do this as a declaration of our union with Jesus:

> *[Love] does not dishonor others, [love] is not self-seeking, [love] is not easily angered, [love] keeps no record of wrongs.*

Jesus does not dishonor others, Jesus is not self-seeking, Jesus is not easily angered, Jesus keeps no record of wrongs.

[Insert your name] does not dishonor others, [insert your name] is not self-seeking, [insert your name] is not easily angered, [insert your name] keeps no record of wrongs.

The Spirit of Jesus lives in you and me. Therefore, we are not destined to live out the habits of our family of origin, repeating the patterns that came naturally as we coped with difficult and traumatic events. We are not bound to actions that flow from insecurity, a need to be noticed, unhealed hurts, or the tendency to hold a grudge.

We can honor others. Instead of disrespecting those around us by not listening well or not being present, we can help people to feel seen, heard, and valued. We can even honor those with whom we disagree, and in so doing help them become tender to an error that may be in their ways. Jesus can do this through us.

We can seek the good of others. We can be those who, when we walk in a room, are known for being encouragers. We can do this because Jesus is helping us become less self-seeking. We are learning the art of cruciform, cross-shaped love in all things, in all contexts. Jesus can do this work in us.

We can be quick to compassion rather than anger. We can enter into the perspective of the other with whom we are talking, catalyzing understanding rather than igniting indignation. We can be those who are quick to understand another, rather than to demand we first be understood. (Consider investing some time in praying the peace prayer of Francis of Assisi for growth in this aspect of love.)

We can be people who are quick to forgive. We can lose track of offenses, remembering the last time the person was good to us rather than the last time they were hurtful. We can treat others as we want to be treated, forgiving as we have been forgiven (Eph. 4:32; Col. 2:13–14).

Union with Jesus means we are maturing in love. It's time to leave some of the baggage of our old ways of loving behind so we can be free to embody the honoring, selfless, compassionate love of Christ.

THE PRAYER

Lord Jesus, I am in you and you are in me. You know that our old habits die hard. But your indwelling Spirit is giving me the power to live in your way of love. Help me to honor others, seek their good, and act with compassion toward them. In Christ Jesus, I pray, amen.

THE QUESTIONS

- What emotions are you quick to respond with in your life right now?

- Have you become slower, over the years of following Jesus, to engage in negative habits?

- Can you celebrate, with Jesus, the progress you have made as he lives in and through you?

IN CHRIST WE LEARN THE WAY OF LOVE (PART FOUR)

1 CORINTHIANS 13:6–7

Love does not delight in evil but rejoices with the truth. It always protects, always trusts, always hopes, always perseveres.

CONSIDER THIS

In union with Jesus, our capacity to live in purity of heart and fullness of hope is realized.

With today's section of 1 Corinthians 13:4–13, let's repeat our exercise of inserting the name of Jesus in the place of love first, and then inserting our own names second as a declaration of our union with Jesus:

Love does not delight in evil but rejoices with the truth. [Love] always protects, [love] always trusts, [love] always hopes, [love] always perseveres.

Jesus does not delight in evil but rejoices with the truth. Jesus always protects, Jesus always trusts, Jesus always hopes, Jesus always perseveres.

[Insert your name] does not delight in evil but rejoices with the truth. [Insert your name] always protects, [insert your name] always trusts, [insert your name] always hopes, [insert your name] always perseveres.

The Spirit of Jesus lives in you and me. Therefore, we are no longer to entertain our old inclinations to lose our moral footing, follow liars, look away from the distressed, mistrust God's goodness, lose hope, or give up easily.

We can rejoice with the truth. Instead of focusing our attention on all the evil we see operating in the world around us, we can give our energies to celebrating what is good, right, and lovely (Phil. 4:8). We can fix our eyes on Jesus and his truth, giving it our best focus (Heb. 12:2). Jesus, living in us, can do this—he can help us see what is right with the world.

We can protect others. We can tend to those who need someone to stand between them and disaster. Jesus, living in us, can make us protectors and guardians of the troubled soul.

We can trust God and others. We can learn to lose our proclivity toward suspicion and negativity and affirm words of confidence in God and belief in others. Jesus, living in us, can help us believe God for miracles and believe that others will come to hope and faith in Christ.

We can hope ceaselessly. We can lean into the promises of God and learn to walk by faith and not by sight. We can become prayer warriors in our prayer closets, those who share the relentless faith of those in the Hall of Faith in Hebrews. We can long for a better country (Heb. 11:16), and speak of it, pray toward it, and embrace its future reality in the present until it comes.

Jesus, living in us, can make us the most hopeful people in our families, in our churches, even in our cities and world.

We can persevere. We can leave our foot on the faith gas pedal, embracing our union with Jesus, as we go through troubles and struggles. We can rehearse that sorrow may last for a night (even a long night), but joy comes in the morning (Ps. 30:5). Jesus, living in us, can turn us away from patterns of giving up in our past and make us people known for our perseverance.

Union with Jesus means that new forms of love, stronger and mightier and more resilient than the weak and feeble forms of love we have left behind, can become our new normal.

THE PRAYER

Lord Jesus, I am in you and you are in me. I am capable of becoming love—like you. By your Spirit today, I will lean into the reality that I am a 1 Corinthians 13 saint because of your transforming work within me. In Christ Jesus, I pray, amen.

THE QUESTIONS

- How is your trust level these days? Do you believe God has your heart, has your back, and has your best in mind as you walk forward into the unknown? Take your trust-pulse, and talk about what you would like Christ in you to do so you can go to the next level of trusting him.

IN CHRIST WE LEARN THE WAY OF LOVE (PART FIVE)

1 CORINTHIANS 13:8A

Love never fails.

CONSIDER THIS

In union with Jesus, you have the God Who Never Fails with you—at all times.

With today's section of 1 Corinthians 13:4–13, let's repeat our exercise of inserting the name of Jesus in the place of love first, and then inserting our own names second as a declaration of our union with Jesus:

Love never fails.
Jesus never fails.
[Insert your name] never fails.

Here we are, saying things that feel so far beyond us we may feel like we are ignoring reality and confessing positive thoughts that have no weight behind them.

We are doing anything but that.

It is true that Jesus never fails. And because Jesus lives in you, it can be said of you that you never fail. But what happens when someone who never fails, *fails*?

There is a biblical path for those who fail along the way to Christlikeness. It is not the path of wallowing in our brokenness and giving up on being like Jesus. The biblical path forward begins with reclaiming who we are in Christ. Then, having owned our union with Christ and our belovedness to Christ, we move in radical humility. We confess our sin, we repent, we receive grace and forgiveness, and we realign ourselves with the way of Jesus. All of this happens in community.

In other words, your failings inform your *testimony* rather than define your *destiny*.

When I think of Jesus never failing us even in our weakness, I often think of Saint Patrick. As his story goes, he was taken as a slave by Irish raiders from his home in Britain. In his *Confessio*, Patrick talks about how little faith he had and how wayward from God he had become. He spent six years feeding animals until, through a dream, God spoke to him about a ship that was ready for his rescue. After a two-hundred-mile trip, he made it to the ship and sailed to freedom.

Back in Britain, he had a dream in which he heard the "Voice of the Irish" beckoning him back to those who enslaved him. He returned as a missionary to Ireland and the rest is history. If even half of the stories we read about Patrick are true, he had a mighty force of faith—despite his weakness—that flowed from his awareness of his union with Christ. He walked boldly through the land of his pain with wild courage—leading many souls to Jesus.

His sense of union with Christ is captured in a few phrases from his famous prayer *St. Patrick's Breastplate*: "Christ with me, Christ before me, Christ behind me, Christ within me, Christ beneath me, Christ above me, Christ at my right, Christ at my left . . ."

Let's read Paul's words in Ephesians 1:7–12 to remind us of the new reality in which we live in union with Christ Jesus:

> In him we have redemption through his blood, the forgiveness of sins, in accordance with the riches of God's grace that he lavished on us. With all wisdom and understanding, he made known to us the mystery of his will according to his good pleasure, which he purposed in Christ, to be put into effect when the times reach their fulfillment—to bring unity to all things in heaven and on earth under Christ.

In him we were also chosen, having been predestined according to the plan of him who works out everything in conformity with the purpose of his will, in order that we, who were the first to put our hope in Christ, might be for the praise of his glory.

Hallelujah! The God Who Never Fails is the God who chose you. He predestined you to be conformed to Christ Jesus (Rom. 8:29). He invited you into hope in Christ for his praise and ultimate glory. This is the God who lives in you!

A friend once told me after a particularly hard season of ministry, "Dan, success and failure are events, not people." I took a deep breath then, and I invite you to take one with me now.

Jesus is living in you. And you are living in Jesus. This means that God's never-failing nature is in you. Jesus will help you succeed in becoming a person of never-failing love.

THE PRAYER

Lord Jesus, I am in you and you are in me. If I have seen myself as a failure before, I choose to change who I see in the mirror from now on. Your love never fails. You never fail. You in me never fail. I take hold of this truth and make it my own. In Christ Jesus, I pray, amen.

THE QUESTIONS

- How many times have you failed in your life? And how many times have you gotten back up to try again? What has the Lord taught you about himself, and yourself, in that process?

36

IN CHRIST WE LEARN THE WAY OF LOVE (PART SIX)

1 CORINTHIANS 13:8b–12a

But where there are prophecies, they will cease; where there are tongues, they will be stilled; where there is knowledge, it will pass away. For we know in part and we prophesy in part, but when completeness comes, what is in part disappears. When I was a child, I talked like a child, I thought like a child, I reasoned like a child. When I became a man, I put the ways of childhood behind me. For now we see only a reflection as in a mirror; then we shall see face to face.

CONSIDER THIS

Just thirty minutes of watching the Academy Awards or the Grammy Awards will make it clear. We live in a day and in a culture where the talented, impressive, skilled, and passionate are elevated in status.

We put their faces on billboards, pay them well, and gape, scream, or bow when they walk out on a red carpet. We make celebrities out of the capable and confident, and heroes out of actors, actresses, athletes, musicians, and politicians—many whose lives may ring hollow when it comes to Christlike love.

As for the rest of us who live outside of the brightest limelight, we are subtly encouraged to show off our talents and skills in order to step into a little limelight all our own. It almost goes without saying that people should see just how remarkable we are, and give us praise.

In the body of Christ, there are versions of this social malady that can creep in and erode our capacity to live wholly in fellowship with Christ and one another. Celebrity culture can manifest itself as blatant elevation of one Christian leader's personality and teaching over another, or it can manifest itself in what we might call "spiritual one-upmanship" in the local church.

For example, "My spiritual giftedness is better than your spiritual giftedness." We may never say that out loud, but the idea may still have a hold on our hearts as we swim in today's cultural waters.

Paul knew the Corinthian tendency to be led astray by false idols (1 Cor. 12:2). He also knew that they tended to miss Christ as they followed Christian leaders (1 Cor. 1:11–13). Both of these tendencies characterize our age as well.

To address these and other issues with the Corinthians, Paul decides that he will pause in his explanations of spiritual gifts in 1 Corinthians 12 to give a family lesson on how love works in chapter 13. Paul is convinced that Christ lives within us, and from that vantage point, he speaks truth to the subtle corruptions of the heart so common to us.

In 1 Corinthians 12:31b and 13:8, Paul contextualizes all spiritual gifts in their relationship to the "most excellent way": love. For Paul, without Christ's love at work in us, spiritual gifts can mesmerize us into believing they are the point—rather than the pointer. Gifts are intended to point to *love*.

In other words, Paul puts loving well in a higher spiritual category than expressing gifts well or performing well.

Prophecies? They will end. Tongues? They'll be stilled. Knowledge? It will go away. In each case, prefaced by the statement, "Love never fails" (v. 8), public displays of spiritual or intellectual prowess are categorized as temporal and limited.

But love? It is *eternal*.

Love is the quality of a Christian in his or her most mature and complete state. The spiritually immature

   DAN WILT

may talk about spiritual gifts as if they are the sign and signal of Christian maturity.

No, Paul says. Only love is the mark of full maturity in Christ.

To become a vessel of love means that we must put away childish things. As a pastor, I watched this affection for stages and visibility (rationalized and perpetuated even by leaders in the name of reach and influence) confuse many. Please don't get me wrong. We need well-known saints. We need strong, faithful, and visible leaders. We need to do things well, serve with great acts of creative excellence, and curate platforms for faithful messages.

What we don't need is for the church to make celebrities of people, making them out to be somehow more valuable to God or us than the hidden saint who is faithfully caring for one person in loving obedience to Christ.

We must put childish ways behind us. We see through a glass dimly for now, but one day we will see the fullness of Love blazing in all his eternal glory. Then we will understand. Then all the things we now celebrate with such zeal will come into perspective.

In union with Jesus, we will learn the humble and hidden art of loving well, the most supreme of all kingdom activities.

Today, you and I can welcome Jesus to stir our hearts to appreciate what will truly last—acts of love touching hearts in the name of Jesus.

THE PRAYER

Lord Jesus, I am in you and you are in me. If I have elevated more public gifts, either in my own life or by over-celebrating them in others, please wash my heart clean. I want to love in your way, according to your nature. Love through me, Jesus. Love through me. In Christ Jesus, I pray, amen.

THE QUESTIONS

- Have you ever found yourself comparing yourself to someone more outwardly gifted, minimizing the work of God in you because of that comparison?

- What could you do, today, to put loving well in a higher category than performing well?

37

IN CHRIST WE LEARN THE WAY OF LOVE (PART SEVEN)

1 CORINTHIANS 13:12B–13

Now I know in part; then I shall know fully, even as I am fully known. And now these three remain: faith, hope and love. But the greatest of these is love.

CONSIDER THIS

Revelation is a powerful experience. One moment you're sure you know everything there is to know about someone or something, then, in the next instant, a truth is revealed that changes the course of your life. It's a *revelation*, from the root meaning "to reveal"—and it can be life-altering.

For some of us, coming to Jesus, or experiencing a moment of awakening to his love along our journey, was like that. One minute we knew him one way, and in the next, we were undone by a revelation of his person and glory. When we became aware that we had passed from one understanding of Jesus to another, we may have experienced an overwhelming sense of joy and humility. Recalling these times of God's self-revealing can help us move away from residual, habitual, know-it-all attitudes to a renewed humility toward God and others.

I've always loved how C. S. Lewis described his conversion in his book *Surprised by Joy*. He writes about a trip during which he had a simple revelation:

> When we set out I did not believe that Jesus Christ is the Son of God, and when we reached the zoo I did. Yet I had not exactly spent the journey in thought. Nor in great emotion. . . . It was more like when a man, after long sleep, still lying motionless in bed, becomes aware that he is now awake.[11]

Lewis was describing his awakening to Jesus as an epiphany that was a long time in the making.

In 1 Corinthians 13:12b–13, Paul brings his chapter on love to a reflective conclusion: "Now I know in part; then I shall know fully, even as I am fully known" (v. 12b).

---

11. C. S. Lewis, *Surprised by Joy: The Shape of My Early Life* (1955; repr., New York: HarperOne, 2017), 290.

His words speak of a reality that seems inherent to so much of his writing. He has received revelation from the Holy Spirit, but we sense that he knows there is so much more to come. For that reason, he writes with an undercurrent of humility. He seems to know that God could surprise him with another layer of insight at any moment.

Today's passage has the fragrance of great humility and hope. Paul is aware, even knowing he has the mind of Christ (1 Cor. 2:16), that he knows the love of God "in part." Paul knows that his revelation of Jesus and his love will one day come into a great and astounding fullness.

We hear the beautiful reach for the "fullness of God" (Eph. 3:19) in his words when he writes about love. At times, he begins to shift almost into poetry and lyric as he writes words like: "For I am convinced that neither death nor life, neither angels nor demons, neither the present nor the future, nor any powers, neither height nor depth, nor anything else in all creation, will be able to separate us from the love of God that is in Christ Jesus our Lord" (Rom. 8:38–39).

We hear the brimming gratitude in his voice as he writes: "I have been crucified with Christ and I no longer live, but Christ lives in me. The life I now live in the body, I live by faith in the Son of God, who loved me and gave himself for me" (Gal. 2:20).

And here, at the conclusion of his great chapter on love, Paul communicates that there is a revelation of

Jesus, of love, to come. It will be a watershed moment in which he will intimately and fully know the one who has loved him, just as he has been fully known by him. Love will come to its fullness. And if you follow Jesus today, you can expect this culminating revelation of God and his love for yourself as well.

I would encourage you to take time today to imagine the moment ahead when the veil is lifted and you see Jesus face-to-face. Like Lewis in his moment of simple revelation, we will shift from one state to another, from one posture of worship to another. Perhaps that new state of being will be indescribable as we gaze on the beauty of the one with whom we are united (Rom. 6:5; 1 Cor. 6:17).

In verse 13, Paul talks about faith, hope, and love in contrast with one another. Our assurance of things hoped for—*faith* (Heb. 11:1)—our trust in the eternal that is unseen—*hope* (2 Cor. 4:16–18)—will not compare to the eternal joy we will experience when love, in all its fullness, is revealed to us. Along the way, Christ's love is what changes us, leads us, and forms the essential foundation for the gospel (John 3:16). His love is what compels us to serve others (2 Cor. 5:14–15) and leads them to trust in Jesus.

Fullness of love is the culmination of union with God in Christ. Love will "last into God's new world."[12]

---

12. N. T. Wright, *Paul for Everyone: 1 Corinthians* (London: Westminster John Knox Press, 2004), 179.

In union with Christ, we can know love in a profound and increasing way as God's Spirit moves within us. And there is a day coming, a day when every tear will be wiped away (Rev. 21:3–4), when we will see Jesus as he is. We will see him face-to-face.

On that day, we will know love in its fullness. We will know fully, even as we are fully known.

THE PRAYER

Lord Jesus, I am in you and you are in me. I enter into your love story with me and with your people in a new way each day. Help me to pursue love. It is the "most excellent way" to live, and it is the goal of my faith—union with you and the fullness of your love. In Christ Jesus, I pray, amen.

THE QUESTIONS

- Can you name a time when you knew something in part, but then it was revealed to you fully? How did that moment feel?

- Have you ever meditated on this passage before? As you sit with it now, what do you think it means that the "greatest of these is love"?

38

IN CHRIST GOD'S PROMISES ARE FULFILLED

2 CORINTHIANS 1:20

For no matter how many promises God has made, they are "Yes" in Christ. And so through him the "Amen" is spoken by us to the glory of God.

CONSIDER THIS

Promises, promises. Standing in our kitchen with my wife and daughter, two of the three of us agreed that I had made the promise. I didn't remember making it. But when two of the brightest women in your life, who both have strong memories, are telling you that you made a promise to buy your daughter a new laptop for her high school graduation—you *listen*.

Being a keeper of promises is what I hope to be known for in my home and in my lifetime. I can hope to become that kind of man because the ultimate Keeper of Promises lives in me.

The same is true of you. The Keeper of Promises has made promises throughout history, and throughout your life and mine, that he is bringing to fruition. Unlike me, he doesn't forget what he has promised. And "in Christ," he says a resounding yes to all those promises he has made to his people. According to today's verse, through him, and being found in him (Phil. 3:9a), we offer our hearty amen!

In Christ, God's promises are fulfilled for us.

There is the promise of *habitation*—Jesus abides in us and we abide in Jesus (John 15:4–5) by the promised Holy Spirit (Eph. 1:13–14).

There is the promise of *participation*—we are identified with Christ in his life, death, and resurrection (Rom. 6:5–8). The covenant with the Father is fulfilled for us all in Christ and we are reconciled to God (2 Cor. 5:18–19).

There is the promise of *incarnation*—we are maturing toward a place where our union with Jesus comes to its fruition and we can say confidently with Paul, "I no longer live, but Christ lives in me" (Gal. 2:20).

We are seeing the fulfillment of Joel 2:28–29, where God promises that he would pour out his Spirit on all people (Acts 2:16–21). We are seeing the fulfillment of

Jesus's promise that the love the Father has for Jesus would be in us, and Jesus himself would be in us (John 17:26).

In our Prayer of Union and Love in Ephesians 3:14–21, Paul prays for us "to know this love that surpasses knowledge—that you may be filled to the measure of all the fullness of God" (v. 19). Peter echoes the purpose of God's promises in 2 Peter 1:4: "He has given us his very great and precious promises, so that through them you may participate in the divine nature."

You and I are being invited to participate in the divine nature. We are invited to know this love that surpasses all knowledge and to be filled to the measure of the fullness of God. Your union is with Jesus, who is in you and is making the promises behind these invitations come to pass.

Today, we can revel in the promises of God. One way to do this is to get one of those handy lists or card decks that lays out the promises of God in the Scriptures. Using tools like these, we can recite and memorize great and precious promises that are our inheritance every single day.

Another way to revel in the promises of God is to follow the liturgical calendar, or what we call the Awakening Calendar. This rhythm keeps us focusing on the promises of God through seasons like Advent, Christmas, Lent, Easter, and more.

We could even call this way of marking time the Promise Calendar! Tish Harrison Warren writes:

> The liturgical calendar reminds us that we are people who live by a different story. And not just by a story, but in a story. God is redeeming all things, and our lives—even our days—are part of that redemption. . . . Redemption is crashing into our little stretch of the universe, bit by bit, day by day, mile by coming mile. We have hope because our Lord has promised that he is preparing a place for us. We are waiting, but we will make it home.[13]

If we live in the *story* of God, we live in the *promises* of God.

Take heart today. God's great yes is resounding to you as his child. In Christ, you are the recipient of grace upon grace (John 1:16–18). Like my daughter with her laptop, you are receiving what was promised because that is what love does. You are receiving the goal of your faith—the salvation of your soul (1 Peter 1:8–9).

---

13. Tish Harrison Warren, *Liturgy of the Ordinary: Sacred Practices in Everyday Life* (Downers Grove: InterVarsity Press, 2016), 113–14.

THE PRAYER

Lord Jesus, I am in you and you are in me. You are the fulfiller of the promises you have made. I remember each one, and will gather them for remembrance so that I can praise you for all you have done, are doing, and are going to do. In Christ Jesus, I pray, amen.

THE QUESTIONS

- What promises in the Scriptures is God fulfilling?

- What promises in your own life, promises you believe God gave to you, is he fulfilling?

- What is the part you have to play in seeing those promises come to fulfillment?

39

IN CHRIST WE ARE A NEW CREATION

2 CORINTHIANS 5:17

Therefore, if anyone is in Christ, the new creation has come: The old has gone, the new is here!

CONSIDER THIS

Have you ever been in a butterfly sanctuary? Hundreds of butterflies are floating in the air above you and around you. Then—if you are very still—one or more may actually land on you.

This remarkable little aviator, this magnificent, airborne wonder with such vibrant, technicolor wings was, just a short time before, a tiny, slow, wingless caterpillar. Happily munching on leaves and possibly wondering what that colorful being hovering above it might be (or so my imagination tells me), that little larva looks virtually nothing like what it will look like after its metamorphosis.

Being in Christ, and Christ being in us, means we are in the process of *transformation*. Just like that butterfly, we are becoming something that is beyond what we have known before. Our new set of clothing (Gal. 3:27) will be quite remarkable to the world as well.

I have seen some incredible transformations of people who have come to Christ. They shock their friends and family members with their newfound life in Jesus. To stretch the metaphor, entire families of caterpillars have become butterflies—all because one of them put their trust in Christ.

In 2 Corinthians 3:18 we read these words: "And we all, who with unveiled faces contemplate the Lord's glory, are being transformed into his image with ever-increasing glory, which comes from the Lord, who is the Spirit."

The Spirit of the New Creation, the God who makes all things new (Rev. 21:5), lives in you. This is your experiential reality. This is union with God in Christ.

When we see sin in our lives and grieve over it—that is the Spirit at work. If we didn't grieve, if we didn't see our sin as a problem or understand it to be missing the mark of God's best, then we would never be free of it.

When chains of the heart remain, it is like we are a caterpillar, latched onto the branch. We are a small and

     DAN WILT

spiritually flightless version of the human being we were intended to be.

But those who Christ sets free, are free indeed (John 8:36)!

We are free—to fly.

In union with Jesus, you are a new creation. The old is gone; the new has come. In a way, we are both the butterfly and the caterpillar in the chrysalis at the same time. We are positionally a new creation in Christ. The transformation has happened. We are also experientially in process—we are being changed from glory to glory as we practice the way of Jesus and rehearse the way of love, each and every day.

Union with Christ means that we are both a new creation and we are a new creation in process. We can get lost in how difficult that process of transformation can be. A chrysalis can become a womb or a tomb for a caterpillar.

In Christ, he makes it a womb of new and everlasting life. This is the resurrection life he promised because he *is* the resurrection and the life (John 11:25–26). No one can take that reality away from you or me. Jesus is the one who holds the keys of hell and death (Rev. 1:18)—and that means liberty for us all.

Today, Jesus, the resurrection and the life, is in union with your spirit. You have the transforming life of God at work in you. Open yourself to all that Jesus wants to give,

and remove from, your life. Transformation takes both—
and the goal is worth it.

You are a new creation in Christ.

It's time to *fly*.

THE PRAYER

Lord Jesus, I am in you and you are in me. The old has gone, and the new is here. I embrace your new-creation life at work in me, and I want to be transformed. I don't want to stay as I am. I want to become like you in all the ways you desire. In Christ Jesus, I pray, amen.

THE QUESTIONS

- What points of transformation in your own life, or the life of another, painted a true picture of someone being one thing and then becoming a new creation in Christ?

- How can you participate in Christ making you new in areas that feel old and stuck in your heart?

     DAN WILT

40

IN CHRIST WE ARE RECONCILED AND RECONCILERS

2 CORINTHIANS 5:18–21

All this is from God, who reconciled us to himself through Christ and gave us the ministry of reconciliation: that God was reconciling the world to himself in Christ, not counting people's sins against them. And he has committed to us the message of reconciliation. We are therefore Christ's ambassadors, as though God were making his appeal through us. We implore you on Christ's behalf: Be reconciled to God. God made him who had no sin to be sin for us, so that in him we might become the righteousness of God.

CONSIDER THIS

Over the decades, one of my favorite experiences as a pastor has been seeing people come to faith in Jesus. For we who have known what it is to be reconciled to God through Jesus, gratitude fills our hearts daily. When someone else experiences that same welcome from Jesus and responds, it is cause for great rejoicing in the body of Christ.

According to 2 Corinthians 5:19, in Christ, God has done something for the world. God has *reconciled* people to himself. He has made a way for a broken relationship to be made whole, through the death of Jesus on the cross (Col. 1:20). In this great act of reconciliation, God has made a way for anyone—literally, *anyone*—to come into union with him.

God is a *reconciler.*

Coming into union with God in Christ is reconciliation in its most essential form. Any reconciliation we may do on earth that does not find its source and strength in God's greater, reconciling work of the heart to himself is destined to struggle and fall short.

God knows that if he can get a heart relating to him again, experiencing his presence, love, forgiveness, acceptance, and truth, the possibilities of reconciliation between that person and others are *endless.* We who have been reconciled to God begin to want others to be reconciled to God. We want others to experience the freedom that we have experienced. It is the natural flow of the story.

And that is why sharing the good news of reconciliation is our ministry. Just as one who is forgiven much loves much (Luke 7:47), so, too, we who have experienced God closing the gap between us and him want to help close that gap for others.

Every Spirit-filled and Spirit-formed follower of Jesus who carries his heart in the world is an agent of reconciliation between God and people. As God has forgiven us, we can forgive others (Col. 3:13). As God has accepted us, we can accept others (Rom. 15:7).

Someone moving as an emotionally and relationally healthy person in the world, embodying a life reconciled to God and committed to reconciliation between people, is a powerful witness. Few homes or businesses see that kind of character evidenced in a person on a daily, weekly, or even yearly basis.

It is Christ shining through our eyes and actions who is doing the reconciling.

In union with Jesus, as one to whom the message of reconciliation has been committed, begin to see yourself as an agent of reconciliation today. Instead of seeing evangelism as converting someone to a set of beliefs, see your primary work as helping a person become reconciled to the God who is pursuing them. Loving someone well, with Christlike love (1 Corinthians 13), opens the door to all manner of reconciliation.

God has made a way for you and me to be in relationship with him. And that relationship is the best thing that ever happened to us.

Now we have a chance to both participate in seeing others reconciled to God and to celebrate with those who have responded to the reconciliation God offers. We could run our prayer life with prayers for reconciliation between God and people for decades. God brings hearts to himself in surprising ways when his people pray. I have many people that I am praying for to be reconciled to God. I know the burdens that will be lifted off of their hearts when they are.

As Christ's ambassador, Jesus is making his appeal through you to others. He is calling them to be reconciled to God. Pray, step out the door, set your heart to love others with the love of Christ, and look for anyone he sends you.

THE PRAYER

Lord Jesus, I am in you and you are in me. First, I want to have the path of my heart clear between us. If there is any area in which I am holding back, show me so I can give it to you and receive your reconciling love and forgiveness. Second, I want to be a reconciler, a true peacemaker (Matt. 5:9) in my sphere of relationships. Show me the way. In Christ Jesus, I pray, amen.

THE QUESTIONS

- Do you feel like there is a clear and open relational path between you and the Father? If so, talk about your relationship with God at this time in your life. If not, how could you consecrate yourself to God to a new degree and open up the path?

41

IN CHRIST WE HAVE
A NEW IDENTITY

GALATIANS 2:20

I have been crucified with Christ and I no longer live, but Christ lives in me. The life I now live in the body, I live by faith in the Son of God, who loved me and gave himself for me.

CONSIDER THIS

At the beginning of the security line in virtually every major airport is a security guard checking passports. The official looks down at the document, back up at you (recently some airports ask you to look into a camera), and either confirms your entry or asks you to step aside.

In that context, a passport validates who you are, where you are from, and if you are an upstanding passenger. Once approved, I have often experienced guards in US airports pausing to say something to the effect of, "Enjoy your flight, [insert your name]." That last part always feels good; it almost makes it worth the wait in line. Almost.

In Galatians 2:20, Paul articulates the details on the Christian passport for life in Christ. You could almost hear him saying in any place where his true identity is being reviewed, "I no longer live, but Christ lives in me." While the phrase "in Christ" does not appear in this verse, this is a true "union with God in Christ" passage.

Sitting at the heart of Paul's theology and vision of the gospel, this verse is a crystallization of Paul's deepest belief about our identity as Christians—those who he says are "in Christ." We are no longer identified with the law (Gal. 2:19) or who we were before we met Christ (Eph. 4:22–24).

We are identified with Christ—even to the degree that Paul will say that Christ is actually the one living through him.

It is here that we must pause in our study of union with God in Christ to embrace a halting reality. Paul is not after us just becoming like Jesus, though he does use this language from time to time. He also does not talk about Jesus as if he is primarily on the outside working on Paul's life.

Paul is identifying himself with the Lord who *inhabits* him, the Spirit who *inhabits* him.

Paul has put every other identity behind him other than Jesus and his belovedness to Jesus. We are called to do the same. Here in Galatians 2:20, he does not define himself by the ideologies, the "-isms," and "-ists" of his day. He aligns himself with Jesus. He belongs to Jesus. He answers only to Jesus. He obeys only Jesus. He does not blend his allegiances; Jesus is the only Lord for Paul. Early Christians were discipled to do the same.

When people look at your spiritual passport, the person looking at you is in for a treat. May they see Jesus—who is in you as you are in him (John 15:4–5). Paul emphasizes this true and profound unity with Christ as he places himself with Jesus in his crucifixion, participating with Jesus in his crucifixion. Because in Adam all die (the first Adam), so in Christ we are all made alive (the Second Adam) (1 Cor. 15:22, 42–45).

Paul has died to his old way of life and the old passports that held his identity. His new passport declares that he is in unity with his crucified master. As one scholar put it: "The cross, like all prophetic and charismatic acts, is a creative event; indeed, it creates a new horizon, a new world."[14] Because of the cross, Paul has a new horizon, a new world—a new self. And so do you and I.

May you be able to say today that you have been crucified with Christ and, "I no longer live, but Christ lives in me." May you be able to say, "The life I now live

---

14. Michael J. Gorman, *Cruciformity: Paul's Narrative Spirituality of the Cross* (Grand Rapids: Wm. B. Eerdmans, 2001, 2021), 383.

in the body, I live by faith in the Son of God, who loved me and gave himself for me."

This is union with God in Christ. This is your new identity.

THE PRAYER

Lord Jesus, I am in you and you are in me. My identity is with you, on the cross. My identity is with you, in your resurrection. I want to embrace this new identity, and to be able to say, "I no longer live, but Christ lives in me." In Christ Jesus, I pray, amen.

THE QUESTIONS

- Can you say that you have put every other identity behind you other than Jesus? Talk about the processes in your life that led you to choose your identity in Christ over other identities that vied for your allegiance.

42

IN CHRIST WE ARE CHILDREN OF GOD

GALATIANS 3:26

So in Christ Jesus you are all children of God through faith.

CONSIDER THIS

Today, you have permission to be a child. Neuroscientists are uncovering that one's ability to play heightens creativity and supports a general sense of well-being. Using our imagination, playing games, playing sports, and more brings good things up in us—and brings bad things down.

You should play more. I should play more. We should *all* play more.

Now, have you ever imagined playing with God? In other words, can you imagine the same delight filling God's heart that fills yours when playing with, reading to, singing with, or watching a child? I like to think that Jesus played with the children and they laughed in his presence.

Could you and I imagine (and yes, there are no verses on this of which I am aware) that God might be young at heart—and aspire to be like him in this? Could we go with God on adventures and plan outings with our Father who loves us?

Jesus was quite clear in Matthew 18:2–5:

> He called a little child to him, and placed the child among them. And he said: "Truly I tell you, unless you change and become like little children, you will never enter the kingdom of heaven. Therefore, whoever takes the lowly position of this child is the greatest in the kingdom of heaven. And whoever welcomes one such child in my name welcomes me."

Healthy children are humble, expectant, accepting, quick to love, and ready to believe they are capable of almost anything. Children are also not in a hurry, at least not like adults are. That is because the hurry is not yet in them. They tend to savor life, rather than gulp it down.

I remember my own son, when he was small, stopping on a walk to watch a caterpillar crawl across the path. We were in a hurry to get to our destination. We turned around to find him down on his haunches transfixed by the colorful bug. We slowed down and joined him. For him, enjoying creation was the destination. (Interestingly enough, it still is.)

It is "adulting" (as my children call it), and the challenges and messages that come to us as we age, that slowly draw us away from that childlike state before God and others.

In Christ, we are God's children. In the Old Testament, Israel was understood to be God's child (Ex. 4:22). In the New Testament, John reminds us: "Yet to all who did receive him, to those who believed in his name, he gave the right to become children of God— children born not of natural descent, nor human decision or a husband's will, but born of God" (John 1:12–13).

And what a profound metaphor this is that God chose. The child belongs to the parent, and the parent belongs to the child. They are intended to be joined in the most beautiful way; the child nurtured within the parent's loving care and the parent delighted by the child's growth.

The Father's table in the Father's house is large and inviting; no background or ethnicity precludes anyone from the table who wants to be there.

To be a beloved daughter, a beloved son, is to follow in the path of Jesus. In his baptismal waters, the words of love that rang true for Jesus could be understood to ring true for us as we consider today's verse. An adaptation might be: "This is [my child], whom I love; with [my child] I am well pleased" (adapted from Matt. 3:17). Yes, the words in the gospel were specifically for Jesus. But I also believe that Jesus would say words like this in this same spirit of love to you today.

There is no flourishing in union with Christ without an increasing and healing awareness of our belovedness to him. I am sure I have personally written this at least a hundred times in my life so far—and I'm still looking for ways and opportunities to write it.

I love how Henri Nouwen encouraged us to practice silence in order to perceive the Father's loving voice speaking to us:

> It is not easy to enter into the silence and reach beyond the many boisterous and demanding voices of our world and to discover there the small intimate voice saying: "You are my Beloved Child, on you my favor rests." Still, if we dare to embrace our solitude and befriend our silence, we will come to know that voice . . . a voice that can be heard by the ear of faith, the ear of the inner heart.[15]

It takes faith to become a child. It is through faith that we can achieve it, as we allow God's Spirit within us to restore to us the tenderness and innocence that only a child can have.

---

15. Henri Nouwen, *Life of the Beloved: Spiritual Living in a Secular World* (New York: Crossroad Publishing Company, 1992, printed in 2013), 77.

And if I could add one more thing to today's reflection: perhaps we can learn to play once again, even play with God. He is the Creator of our imaginations, our delights, and our interests. Positionally, before God and before the world, we are God's child by covenant and union.

But also embrace that you are God's child personally and experientially. Seek to live a life full of wonder, with a propensity to play as hard as you work, and with a ceaseless expectation that God's goodness will follow you all the days of your life (Ps. 23:6).

THE PRAYER

Lord Jesus, I am in you and you are in me. I want to become like a little child, living in loving union with you, my Father. I desire that I would grow young in heart, Holy Spirit, even as I age in body. Let it be, for your glory. In Christ Jesus, I pray, amen.

THE QUESTIONS

- When was the last time you really *played*? Is there anything that might be holding you back from delighting in the life God has given you as his child?

- What do you think it means to be a covenant child of God?

- What have you learned so far about the reality that you are God's child?

43

IN CHRIST FAITH IS EXPRESSED THROUGH LOVE

GALATIANS 5:6

For in Christ Jesus neither circumcision nor uncircumcision has any value. The only thing that counts is faith expressing itself through love.

CONSIDER THIS

The other morning I drove by a church in our area that posts a weekly inspirational (or humorous) quote on the sign on their lawn. The letters are plastic and sometimes crooked, but it's clear that someone has carefully curated each word to provide some benefit to those who pass by. This particular day I drove by quickly, almost missing the message. There on the sign were these words: "Love as Jesus loves."

We've already talked much about love in our series so far. Paul won't talk about our unity with God in Christ without bringing it up. Paul won't even talk about being a follower of Jesus without putting our embodiment of Christ's love front and center.

And, in everyday life, love is a word that holds more space in the average person's life than most.

We all want to love and be loved, give love and receive love. But *love*, as a word, can mean many, many things. The ancient Greeks had multiple words for love, enabling them to distinguish between meanings in various contexts. The English language, however, has one word for love and a few other variations at best. That limitation has had tremendous implications for us today.

What we mean by love when we speak of it is everything. In our love-language-saturated world, especially on social media and in our identity-disoriented culture, God's vision of love penetrates and defines the meaning of this powerful little word.

And that is what Paul wants to talk about in Galatians 5:26. Some of the believers have retreated into a *law-powered* vision of closeness with God. Paul wants to remind them of a *love-powered* vision of closeness with God—and the mission of love that flows from it.

"The only thing that counts is faith expressing itself through love."

The word for love here is *agape*. Agape is a Father, Son, and Holy Spirit kind of love that could be understood to enfold and define all other visions of love. It is not simply an emotional love, marked by acceptance, kindness, or affection. Rather, it is an unconditional assignment of value to another, a love that puts others first, that deeply loves and appreciates the depth and breadth of a person. It is cruciform, cross-shaped love; the kind of love that calls another to a higher good at the same time it enfolds them. Agape love can accept, challenge, serve, and heal—all in the same moment.

But what does that love look like in practice? Paul is trying to say that it looks like Jesus. And Jesus, whose Spirit is in us, loves in the way of 1 Corinthians 13 and Galatians 5:22–23. His love overflows into joy, peace, patience, kindness, goodness, faithfulness, gentleness, and self-control. That's the Spirit's life at work within us.

Joe Dongell, in his book *Sola Sancta Caritas*, articulates John Wesley's understanding of how love works:

Wesley is saying something more than that love is important, a claim with which all Christians could agree without dispute. Rather, Wesley has a specific understanding of how love works across the whole Christian life, and how love is the operational center of all things. . . . First, the love advocated by Jesus and his apostles cannot be defined by general human intuition,

                    DAN WILT

or by cultural sensibilities, or by finding some supposed ethical overlap between all the world's religions. . . . Second, we must stop equating Christian love with good actions, even if those good actions are done in the name of Jesus. . . . Third, love's origin is God himself, or as it is expressed in 1 John 4:7, "Love is of God." . . . Fourth, if love is a gift from God, then we must seek to receive love from God, the very love we are commanded then to express both to God and others. . . . Fifth, the love poured out by God through the Spirit is a mighty force set loose on the deepest chambers of the heart and community, manifesting a host of powerful internal and external effects.[16]

Because this book is so helpful to our understanding of love, here is one more quote:

If love fills the heart (and by its nature fulfills the whole law of God), then the heart so filled with love has "no room left in it" (metaphorically speaking) for evil intentions and designs. . . . Then among the external effects of infusion with God's love will be mission and service of every sort. For to be filled with love from God is to

---

16. Joseph Dongell, *Sola Sancta Caritas* (Franklin, TN: Seedbed Publishing, 2006), 25–33.

be energized by the same passion that has been energizing God's whole redemptive mission.[17]

The only thing that ultimately matters, according to Paul, is faith expressing itself in the world by acts of love in accord with a Jesus-kind of love. His love is the way forward for us all.

Today, you can express your faith through acts of love because Jesus is in you—loving others through you.

THE PRAYER

Lord Jesus, I am in you and you are in me. I want my faith and the way I carry it in my relationships to be expressed as love. Show me how to love and accept, but also how to care for and challenge another. I want love and truth to move together in my life. In Christ Jesus, I pray, amen.

THE QUESTIONS

- How have different visions of love impacted your relationships?

- Is there any way you could model a love that is a Jesus-kind of love?

---

17. Dongell, *Sola Sancta Caritas*, 34–35.

  DAN WILT

44

IN CHRIST WE ARE SEATED IN HEAVENLY PLACES

EPHESIANS 2:1, 4–7

As for you, you were dead in your transgressions and sins. . . . But because of his great love for us, God, who is rich in mercy, made us alive with Christ even when we were dead in transgressions—it is by grace you have been saved. And God raised us up with Christ and seated us with him in the heavenly realms in Christ Jesus, in order that in the coming ages he might show the incomparable riches of his grace, expressed in his kindness to us in Christ Jesus.

CONSIDER THIS

Every once in a long while a movie comes out that has everything the viewer wants. This *has-it-all* movie has a compelling story, thrilling adventure, spine-tingling drama, surprising comedy, loyal friendship, blossoming romance, a celebration of family love, striking special effects, and, perhaps best of all, an epic struggle between good and evil. That kind of movie is destined to succeed at the box office.

On May 25, 1977, when I was just a young teenager, my *has-it-all* movie hit the silver screen. I found the ad for it at the bottom of the movie page in the local newspaper, and my father and I went to see it together in a near-empty theater. The name of the obscure, new movie? *Star Wars.* And for a young boy captivated by space and the great beyond, it was just about *perfect.* I can almost hear the beloved character, R2D2, affirming my choice to reference the groundbreaking movie with a "beep-beep-boop-beep."

Today's verse about union with God in Christ and the love God has for us is better as a passage than *Star Wars* as a movie. Why? Because it *is* perfect in so many ways. It is God's Word; it is about his perfect love for us; it is about us becoming perfect in love (Col. 3:14; 1 John 4:18); and it resonates with perfect truths that are keeping the universe on its course.

Ephesians 2:1, 4–7 is a true, *has-it-all* verse. Let's read it out loud again, with enthusiasm:

> *As for you, you were dead in your transgressions and sins. . . . But because of his great love for us, God, who is rich in mercy, made us alive with Christ even when we were dead in transgressions—it is by grace you have been saved. And God raised us up with Christ and seated us with him in the heavenly*

     DAN WILT

realms in Christ Jesus, in order that in the coming ages he might show the incomparable riches of his grace, expressed in his kindness to us in Christ Jesus.

First, we were dead. As a friend put it years ago, "Jesus didn't come to make bad people good. Jesus came to make dead people live." We were dead in our transgressions and sins; our soul was corrupted, and we were in a sleep unto death. Welcome to the world as we know it.

"But . . ."—and here the soundtrack supports the dramatic movement, the sheer romance of the story—"But because of his great love for us, . . ." God acted. From his abounding affection for you, for me, and for the world he loves (John 3:16), God intervened on our behalf.

"God, who is rich in mercy" is a character note about the Trinity, the Divine Hero, of our story. And here come the special effects—". . . made us alive with Christ." Dead hearts come to whole and fulfilling and beautiful life! The epic battle of good and evil presses the scene forward as we read that grace was poured out on us, saving us from the devil's grip on our hearts (1 John 3:8b).

But wait, there's *more!* Just when you think the special effects couldn't get any better . . . POW! "God raised us up with Christ and seated us in the heavenly realms in Christ Jesus." We are *with* Jesus in heaven as we walk on earth. We carry his heavenly perspective with us into the grocery store, into that difficult meeting, into a voting booth, into a room filled with grief or joy.

Can you feel the storyline rising—the adventure, the laughter, the friendship, the abundance of breathtaking kindness—that is in these words?

We are in union with Jesus; we are in Christ Jesus! And in participation with Christ in his death and resurrection (another way of talking about our union with Jesus), God raised us up *with* Christ and seated us in the heavenly realms *in* Christ Jesus.

Once again, union is *habitation* (Christ in you, and you in Christ), *participation* (we died and rose with him), and *incarnation* (Jesus is living his life through us by his Spirit). Today's verse gives us the theological headwaters for these three aspects of our union with Christ, watering them unto blooming and flourishing. Our realized and deepening union with God in Christ is *a result of God's inestimable love for us* (v. 4).

This epic tale is the real one to which all others knowingly or unknowingly point (the "true myth" of Tolkien). The love of God for you, for me, and for the world is at the center of the narrative. The whole plot points back to Jesus.

And finally, why is all this union—this *habitation, participation,* and *incarnation*—necessary? Enter verse 7: "In order that in the coming ages he might show the incomparable riches of his grace, expressed in his kindness to us in Christ Jesus" to a weary world. Can you hear "O Holy Night" playing in the background?

Question: What is the Father's greatest act of kindness to humankind?

Answer: *Christ Jesus is God's greatest act of kindness to humankind.*

You and I, in Christ, are characters in this epic tale of union and love. We are the ones who point the way to the God who is love, the God who is making all things new in Christ.

THE PRAYER

Lord Jesus, I am in you and you are in me. I am thrilled to be a beloved character in your epic story of union and love. I turn my heart toward you today so that I might take my place, showing the same grace to others that you have shown me. In Christ Jesus, I pray, amen.

THE QUESTIONS

- What aspect of today's passage most moves you and why?

- How does seeing yourself as a beloved character in God's epic story of love for humanity help you as you follow him today?

45

IN CHRIST WE BECOME MATURE

EPHESIANS 4:11–16

So Christ himself gave the apostles, the prophets, the evangelists, the pastors and teachers, to equip his people for works of service, so that the body of Christ may be built up until we all reach unity in the faith and in the knowledge of the Son of God and become mature, attaining to the whole measure of the fullness of Christ.

Then we will no longer be infants, tossed back and forth by the waves, and blown here and there by every wind of teaching and by the cunning and craftiness of people in their deceitful scheming. Instead, speaking the truth in love, we will grow to become in every respect the mature body of him who is the head, that is, Christ. From him the whole body, joined and held together by every supporting ligament, grows and builds itself up in love, as each part does its work.

CONSIDER THIS

There is one thing that is true about every child who has ever been born. From the moment of conception, a child *matures*.

Maturity is when one's progress as a human being matches one's reality. Maturity is connected to one's age, perspective, character, relational patterns, and healthy, flourishing human growth. *Immaturity* is a term we use when someone who should be mature enough to act a certain way, live a certain way, speak a certain way, or make choices a certain way does not. An immature person is, in essence, stunted in their growth. And that makes them vulnerable—as well as everyone around them.

Ephesians 4:11–16 has much to say about maturing in Christ.

By Christ's Spirit within us, we are designed to grow, dynamically, as a child grows. We are designed to grow in love, grow in wisdom, and grow in the character of Christ in every way. Maturity is coming into "all the fullness of God" in Christ, according to our Prayer of Union and Love in Ephesians 3:14–21.

Paul follows this prayer in Ephesians 3 with these strong words in Ephesians 4. He is eager for us to come into unity in the faith and in our knowledge of the Son of God so that we might attain the "whole measure of the fullness of Christ" (v. 13).

How does this happen?

First, we need to be filled with the Spirit of God so Jesus is within us, leading us (Eph. 5:18).

Second, we need some long-form discipleship with trusted guides and mentors. Both we and our guides need to go into lifelong training to become like Christ (1 Tim. 4:6–16). We are designed to learn from spiritually gifted guides who will help us mature in Christ (vv. 11–13) as they themselves continue to mature. A trusted guide is not someone who has arrived. A trusted guide is someone who is tender, in public and private, to Jesus's work in their lives. They are becoming more whole as we are becoming more whole.

Those guides should evidence visible maturity in love, maturity in Christlikeness in heart, in mind, in action, in character, as they lead. Whether they are apostles, prophets, evangelists, teachers, preachers, or anything else, all are required to be mature in love.

All guides should evidence they are growing in a depth of union with Christ—the one who defined himself as being "gentle and humble in heart" (Matt. 11:29). The trusted guides you and I choose should be gentle and humble in heart, like their Lord before them, who lives in them.

Discipled by those who are maturing both ahead of us and along with us, our hearts, minds, and attitudes are slowly conformed to Christ (Rom. 8:29) by a process of Spirit-powered transformation.

Then, to put it bluntly, we will cease to be immature.

We won't be gullible, tossed about by every spiritual perspective or idea that comes our way. We will

     DAN WILT

have discernment, godly wisdom, and perspective. We will handle the Word of God correctly, avoiding godless chatter and losing our way in the spiritual noise that stirs in every generation (2 Tim. 2:15–16).

Our ears won't be tickled by new and unusual doctrines, or by the latest teaching—teaching only peripherally rooted in a robust, holistic, biblical vision of Christlikeness (2 Tim. 4:3).

Those living in union with Christ, inhabited by Christ, participating in Christ's life, incarnating his love in the world, will be marked by love. We'll speak the truth in love, as we, his body, become like him, the head of his body (v. 15), the church. We will love as Jesus loves.

We will grow and build one another up in love, the hallmark evidence of our union with God in Christ. We will become *mature*—true saints, holy ones—whose sole purpose in life is no longer to live for ourselves, but to have Christ living his life through us (Gal. 2:20).

THE PRAYER

Lord Jesus, I am in you and you are in me. Maturing in you, coming into the fullness of your life, your heart, and your love, is my great desire. Through trusted guides, and through learning to love and speak the truth in love, conform me completely to you. In Christ Jesus, I pray, amen.

THE QUESTIONS

- How have you matured in Christ over the years?

- What aspects of your discipleship have grown stronger, and what trusted guides have supported you in that journey?

- Are there any areas of your life in which you would like to become more Christlike, and how can you partner with the Holy Spirit in God's intention to make you like Jesus?

DAN WILT

46

IN CHRIST OUR LOVE ABOUNDS

PHILIPPIANS 1:9–11

And this is my prayer: that your love may abound more and more in knowledge and depth of insight, so that you may be able to discern what is best and may be pure and blameless for the day of Christ, filled with the fruit of righteousness that comes through Jesus Christ—to the glory and praise of God.

PHILIPPIANS 2:1–2

Therefore if you have any encouragement from being united with Christ, if any comfort from his love, if any common sharing in the Spirit, if any tenderness and compassion, then make my joy complete by being like-minded, having the same love, being one in spirit and of one mind.

CONSIDER THIS

Philippians. It's a book of *joy*.

The people of Philippi have been very good to Paul. They have shown compassion to him during his imprisonment. His heart is full, his spirit is unchained because of Christ, and his love for God's people is renewed because of the kindness of these precious brothers and sisters.

When one's heart is full, especially in the midst of otherwise challenging circumstances, we experience *joy*.

As Paul writes his letter to the Philippians, it is clear he is full of joy.

In Philippians 1:9–11, he lifts up a prayer that is a companion to his Prayer of Union and Love in Ephesians 3:14–21. In his prayer for the Philippians, he begins, characteristically, with love.

He prays that their love would abound, expand, and flourish with a new depth of understanding and insight. He wants love to become more than a word to them, more even than an action or an idea. He wants love to become their way of seeing God, seeing themselves, seeing people, seeing circumstances, and seeing the whole of creation.

Paul wants them to have a lens of love before them at all times, in all circumstances. Not a sentimental, sappy love devoid of strength and truth and transformation, mind you. He wants them to see as Jesus sees.

Paul wants them to have this lens of love before their eyes so that they can discern what is best and most beautiful in the sight of God. This discernment will inform wise decisions and right actions. Love will be their approach to all things. This, it could be argued, is the aroma of Christ that drew so many to him (2 Cor. 2:15–17). He wants them to fill rooms with the fragrance of God's love.

Seeing through the lens of love is to be their new normal so that they can grow in purity and innocence of spirit, filled with the fruit that comes from relating rightly to God and others.

This, for Paul, would engender praise of the most magnificent and appropriate sort—praise that befits the God who loves us beyond our imagining.

Then, in Philippians 2:1–2, Paul turns to their union with Christ. He knows that joy comes when we are united and moving in step with Jesus at every level of thought, feeling, and action. This is the *telos*, the end goal, of discipleship for Paul. He groans until Christ is formed in them (Gal. 4:19).

He frames his words to graciously exhort them to take a deeper step into the waters of Christlikeness: "If you have any encouragement from being united with Christ, if any comfort from his love, if any common sharing in the Spirit, if any tenderness and compassion, then . . ." What does he ask of them? "Make my joy complete by being like-minded, having the same love [as Jesus], being one in spirit and of one mind [with one another]."

Love-abounding—we see like Jesus.

Like-minded—we think like Jesus.

Of the same love—we feel and act like Jesus.

One in spirit and one of mind—we treat one another as Jesus treated us.

United with Christ—we are people of *joy*.

THE PRAYER

Lord Jesus, I am in you and you are in me. I ask you that my love would abound, more and more, in understanding and insight. I ask you to make me like you, in mind, in love, and in unity with your people. I want to be a person of joy, wherever I go. In Christ Jesus, I pray, amen.

THE QUESTIONS

- What phrase in today's passages moves you, and why?

- What would it mean for you to put on a lens of love today as you go about your normal routine? How might it change your perspective?

47

IN CHRIST WE HAVE BEEN BROUGHT TO FULLNESS

COLOSSIANS 2:9–10A

For in Christ all the fullness of the Deity lives in bodily form, and in Christ you have been brought to fullness.

CONSIDER THIS

Jesus is the whole package.

He is not part of the package, part of the solution, part of the hope. Being in him, living in union with him, and having him dwell within us, is the complete, sufficient, and enduring hope of the human heart.

There is no hope for the heart that matches Jesus. There is no other ultimate solution for the ills of humankind. And no one who has truly discovered the power of Christ's love and the gift of his indwelling and healing presence would want it any other way.

In today's passage, Paul is affirming that Jesus is enough. We are complete in him.

Colossians 2:9–10a is embedded in a broader letter in which Paul is contending for the Colossians to be "encouraged in heart and united in love" so they can know "the mystery of God, namely, Christ, in whom are hidden all the treasures of wisdom and knowledge" (vv. 2–3).

Paul is resisting human philosophies, religious additives, or any other add-ons or just-a-bit-more-ofs that people try to add to their faith in Jesus.

He is clarifying, for the believers, that *Christ is enough.* And they should bristle when anyone suggests otherwise.

In verse 9, Paul affirms that Jesus reigns as the supreme Lord of all. He is completeness itself. He is God incarnate. He is the one in whom "the fullness of the Deity lives in bodily form."

Paul has led us to verse 9 by way of Colossians 1:15–20. Let's read this famous passage out loud together to renew our hope in Christ:

The Son is the image of the invisible God, the first-born over all creation. For in him all things were created: things in heaven and on earth, visible and invisible, whether thrones or powers or rulers or authorities; all things have been created through him and for him. He is before all things, and in him all things hold together. And he is the head of the

DAN WILT

body, the church; he is the beginning and the first-
born from among the dead, so that in everything he
might have the supremacy. For God was pleased to
have all his fullness dwell in him, and through him
to reconcile to himself all things, whether things on
earth or things in heaven, by making peace through
his blood, shed on the cross.

Then, having reminded us of the sufficiency of Jesus in Colossians 2:9, Paul turns toward you and me to remind us of what is real: "And in Christ you have been brought to fullness."

Once again, he comes to verse 10a by way of Colossians 1:25–27. Here, in the language of union, Paul clarifies the mystery that sits at the center of our faith:

> I have become [the church's] servant by the commission God gave me to present to you the word of God in its fullness—the mystery that has been kept hidden for ages and generations, but is now disclosed to the Lord's people. To them God has chosen to make known among the Gentiles the glorious riches of this mystery, which is Christ in you, the hope of glory.

In summary, in Jesus, all the fullness of God dwells (Col. 2:9). In Christ, who dwells within you, you have been brought to fullness (v. 10a).

In other words, we are complete in Christ.

This is not a "Christ and . . ." faith. It is an "in Christ" faith. To be found in Christ is the goal of our faith. Let's not be taken captive by any other cultural or religious narrative that adds to the faith.

God will use many ideas, tools, and people to encourage and build us. But they will be used in our lives by Jesus, at work within us. They are not the point; *he* is. We keep our eyes fixed on him (Heb. 12:2).

Suffering can make us feel as though Jesus is not enough. As you persevere through difficulty, with the supreme Lord of all living and working in you, take encouragement from Paul's words in Romans 5:3–5: "We also glory in our sufferings, because we know that suffering produces perseverance; perseverance, character; and character, hope. And hope does not put us to shame, because God's love has been poured out into our hearts through the Holy Spirit, who has been given to us."

Union with God in Christ, coming into the fullness of his life, will not rescue any of us from suffering. But that does not mean he is not enough or that we are not complete in him.

It means we are on a journey of becoming like him. We are receiving the goal of our faith, the salvation of our souls (1 Peter 1:9).

And there will be grace—sweet, glorious grace all along that narrow way.

     DAN WILT

THE PRAYER

Lord Jesus, I am in you and you are in me. I am grateful that you dwell in me, and that you are transforming me into your likeness through all the trials and suffering I face. I give you thanks for this. Complete your work in me. In Christ Jesus, I pray, amen.

THE QUESTIONS

- How does the picture that Paul paints of Christ in Colossians 1 and 2 move you? Is there a phrase within the passages that encourages you today?

- How has your own suffering caused you to doubt the sufficiency of Christ for you?

- Can you see the fruits of hope, perseverance, and character that have emerged in you as you walk through suffering with Jesus?

48

IN CHRIST WE SET OUR HEARTS AND MINDS ON THINGS ABOVE

COLOSSIANS 3:1–2

Since, then, you have been raised with Christ, set your hearts on things above, where Christ is, seated at the right hand of God. Set your minds on things above, not on earthly things.

CONSIDER THIS

One of the most popular ideas in self-help these days is captured in the word *mindset*. The common encouragement from the personal-makeover mavens and motivational speakers of the age—who dominate social media—is that if you change your mindset you can change your life. While some social media influencers may encourage a person to focus on the wrong things, they are not wrong about this—what you set your mind on can change the course of your life.

Jesus and Paul understood that one's mindset is a powerful thing. Throughout the Gospels, Jesus is helping his listeners change their mindset in verses like Matthew 6:25: "Therefore I tell you, do not worry about your life, what you will eat or drink; or about your body, what you will wear. Is not life more than food, and the body more than clothes?" One could argue that Jesus's entire ministry was a call to change one's mindset about God, oneself, and others.

Paul, following the lead of Jesus in Colossians 3:1–2, talked directly about mindset. But Jesus and Paul did not tell us to set our minds on positive thinking, increasing our influence, or business success. Rather, Jesus and Paul instruct us to get our hearts set and our minds set on *things above*—on the person of Jesus (Heb. 12:2), the love of the Father (1 John 4:16), and life in the Spirit (Gal. 5:25).

First, in verse 1, Paul tells us to get our *hearts* set— fixed on, locked in—on things above. On *Jesus*. And what does Jesus have his heart set on? Loving the Father and loving his people.

We could think of setting our hearts on things above as setting our *affections*, our *desires*, our *loves*, on Jesus. Christ is seated at the right hand of God, so that's where, and toward whom, our desires should be oriented. We are seated in that same heavenly place with Jesus (Eph. 2:6) and, in that place, we have the heart of Christ (Heb. 8:10).

Paul wants us to be *heaven-hearted*, meaning our affections and desires should be set on knowing Christ and the eternal goal of life forever in communion with him. That "heartset" will change how we spend our days, years, or decades.

Second, in verse 2, Paul tells us to get our *minds* set—fixed on, locked in—on things above. On *Jesus*. So what is the mind of Jesus set on? "For the joy set before him he endured the cross, scorning its shame, and sat down at the right hand of the throne of God" (Heb. 12:2b).

Do you remember the temptation in the wilderness when the devil tempted Jesus with the kingdoms of this world and the tiny thrones of those tiny kingdoms? Jesus was seeing another kingdom ahead and his mind was set on the joy before him.

We could think of setting our minds on things above as setting our *thoughts*, our *attitudes*, our *intellect*, on Jesus. Christ is seated at the right hand of God, so that's where, and toward who, our thoughts should be oriented. We are seated in that same heavenly place with him (Eph. 2:6) and, in that place, we have the mind of Christ (1 Cor. 2:16).

Paul wants us to be *heaven-minded*, meaning our thoughts and intentions should be set on thinking the thoughts of Christ and being guided by the Spirit's wisdom in our decisions. That mindset will change how we spend our days, years, and decades.

What is your heart set on today? Through worship, prayer, and intimate communion with Jesus, your heartset can change for the better.

What is your mind set on today? Through Scripture reading, meditation, and learning in fellowship with Jesus, your mindset can change for the better.

In Philippians 4:8, Paul writes: "Finally, brothers and sisters, whatever is true, whatever is noble, whatever is right, whatever is pure, whatever is lovely, whatever is admirable—if anything is excellent or praiseworthy—think about such things." Heart and mind, we can meditate on what leads to love and eternal life.

Jesus is in you, giving you his heart and mind every day. United with him, we can become people whose hearts and minds are fixed on things above—loving and serving others from that place.

THE PRAYER

Lord Jesus, I am in you and you are in me. I set my affections, desires, and loves on you. I set my thoughts, attitudes, and intellect on you. By your Spirit, help me set my heart and mind on things above as I love others in your name. In Christ Jesus, I pray, amen.

- What does it mean to you to have your heart set on things above?

- What does it mean to you to have your mind set on things above?

- What is something you could do today to fix your desires, your thoughts, on Jesus?

49

THE SPIRIT OF UNION AND LOVE

2 TIMOTHY 1:7, 9

For the Spirit God gave us does not make us timid, but gives us power, love and self-discipline. . . . He has saved us and called us to a holy life—not because of anything we have done but because of his own purpose and grace. This grace was given us in Christ Jesus before the beginning of time.

CONSIDER THIS

As we near the end of this season in our journey together, it is clear that we've only begun to scratch the surface of the treasures of union and love that fill the pages of the New Testament. But in Christ, every end is a new beginning—and there is so much more that Jesus will teach us in the years to come.

Let's review for a moment before we look at today's passage. Learning from the Apostle of Union and Love, Paul—who learned from the Lord of Union and Love, Jesus—we have been in the School of Union and Love apprenticing to become Witnesses of Union and Love in the world God loves (John 3:16)!

And, of course, virtually none of Paul's language about union and love is solely about us as individuals, though that is indeed an important part of the story. United with Christ, in Christ, we are becoming a Community of Union and Love in the world. We are the body of Christ—embodying and evidencing the profound mystery of his love (1 Cor. 13:1–13)—that the world may know Jesus is Lord to the glory of God the Father.

Writing to Timothy, Paul gives us two high vantage points from which to look out over all we have discovered together—the vantage points of the Spirit and grace.

Second Timothy 1:7, 9 is a duet of passages unveiling the character of the Spirit indwelling us and the grace so freely given to us by the Father in Jesus.

In verse 7, we see that the Spirit that is in you and me is known for power, love, and self-discipline. I like to think of the Spirit as the Spirit of Union and Love. Therefore, today we live in union with Jesus as people who are also known for power, love, and self-discipline. That power abides in you. That love abides in you. That self-discipline abides in you.

 DAN WILT

The Spirit that is in you and me is not known for timidity, indifference, or a lack of self-control. Therefore, those whom Christ inhabits are not to be known for those things. The indwelling Jesus is moving through us for a purpose—that we and the world may know and experience the purest love that sets all worlds right. That means that our transformation into Christlikeness is the way the world will be reached.

In verse 9, we see that this grace, given to us "in Christ Jesus," means that we have been filled with God's presence and love not because we did something right, but because God acted in love. As beloved sons and daughters, we have been loved, healed, strengthened, forgiven, renewed, blessed, and sanctified because of the Father's relentless care.

Of the more than one hundred times the phrase "in Christ" or a variation of it is used, the phrase in this passage reminds us that God's intention to bring us into union with himself has been in motion from before the beginning of time.

The Spirit is strong in you. Grace has brought you here.

This is your reality and mine.

There will always be more to learn, but with the Spirit of power, love, and self-discipline within us, and the lavish, abundant grace afforded us, we will come "to know this love that surpasses knowledge" and be "filled to the measure of all the fullness of God" (Eph. 3:19).

THE PRAYER

Lord Jesus, I am in you and you are in me. Your Spirit in me means that I am free to live in power, love, and self-discipline. I choose to live in and from the abundant grace you have shown me. Your Spirit is strong within me and your grace has brought me to this moment. Thank you. I bless your name. In Christ Jesus, I pray, amen.

THE QUESTIONS

- What does having the Spirit of power, love, and self-discipline within mean to you?

- How would you describe God's grace at work in your life?

- Can you think of specific moments or instances in which you felt his grace and unconditional love carrying you through a difficult season?

TO KNOW THIS LOVE

EPHESIANS 3:14–21

For this reason I kneel before the Father, from whom every family in heaven and on earth derives its name. I pray that out of his glorious riches he may strengthen you with power through his Spirit in your inner being, so that Christ may dwell In your hearts through faith. And I pray that you, being rooted and established in love, may have power, together with all the Lord's holy people, to grasp how wide and long and high and deep is the love of Christ, and to know this love that surpasses knowledge—that you may be filled to the measure of all the fullness of God.

Now to him who is able to do immeasurably more than all we ask or imagine, according to his power that is at work within us, to him be glory in the church and in Christ Jesus throughout all generations, for ever and ever! Amen.

CONSIDER THIS

Remember the story of the mourning dove with which we began our journey together? The way to our destination of living in the abundant life and love that is our inheritance in Christ is by deepening in our union with Jesus. It is the only way to full, human flourishing. Our best efforts will not get us where we hope to go. We simply cannot work our way into spiritual vitality and effectiveness. It is in union with Jesus that you and I will thrive in faith, in hope, and in love. Being *in Christ,* and with *Christ in us,* we can experience the fullness of life that Jesus promised.

With the Spirit of Union and Love living within you, within me, we now come full circle back to our Prayer of Union and Love. We entered this season of new-creation growth together by praying the words of Ephesians 3:14–21. Today we will do the same as we mingle our prayers with the saints across the ages who have prayed this prayer in their own times and places.

Pray these words for the body of Christ, for the saints in your local community, for yourself, and for those God has placed in love's reach of you. Let's go back to the prayer as we personalized it at the beginning:

> *I/we kneel before you, Father, from whom every family in heaven and on earth derives its name. I/ we pray that out of your glorious riches you would strengthen me/us with power through your Spirit in my/our inner being, so that Christ may dwell in my/our heart(s) through faith. And I pray that I/ we, being rooted and established in love, may have*

     DAN WILT

power, together with all the Lord's holy people, to grasp how wide and long and high and deep is the love of Christ, and to know this love that surpasses knowledge—that I/we may be filled to the measure of all the fullness of God. Now to you who are able to do immeasurably more than all we ask or imagine, according to your power that is at work within me/ us, to you be glory in the church and in Christ Jesus throughout all generations, for ever and ever! Amen.

To know this love that surpasses knowledge, to be filled to the measure of all the fullness of God, is the goal of our faith. We are becoming those who live in perfect union with God in Christ, both positionally and experientially. We will attain that goal by grace as we humbly receive power from the Holy Spirit to live from, into, and with Christ. We do this by exercising our faith in God to do what he has promised.

As we conclude our meditation on union and love, let me offer a few pastoral words.

For our part, faith is at the center of living in union with Jesus.

This will always be a walk by faith, and not by sight (2 Cor. 5:7). When we feel as though Christ is in us, the hope of glory, he is (Col. 1:27). When we don't feel as though Christ is in us, the hope of glory, he still is! That is how "confidence in what we hope for and assurance about what we do not see" works (Heb. 11:1).

Faith in Jesus, even when we do not see or feel his presence with us, is a key to Christian living. For that reason, faith is a guiding element in Paul's prayer (Eph. 3:17a).

We will persevere through trials and troubles by Jesus's Spirit within us giving us strength. It is in our perfect union with Jesus that we as children are made whole, hopeful, and are renewed inwardly day by day (2 Cor. 4:16–18).

We can also rehearse our union with God in Christ daily and weekly. We can put in our calendar opportunities for our love for God and others to be renewed. We can plan in personal and public worship, caring for others, and banded relationships. We can spend time meditating on the truth of our union privately and with others by reading the Scriptures, investing daily time in prayer, receiving good mentoring and teaching from trusted guides, and more.

I would encourage you to become a lifelong learner about what it means to be "in Christ," and to have Christ in you. The one who began this good work in you will be faithful to complete it to the day of Christ Jesus (Phil. 1:6).

I conclude by praying Ephesians 3:17b–19 specifically for you: "And I pray that you, being rooted and established in love, may have power, together with all the Lord's holy people, to grasp how wide and long and

 DAN WILT

high and deep is the love of Christ, and *to know this love* that surpasses knowledge—that you may be filled to the measure of all the fullness of God" (emphasis mine).

Grace and Peace to you.

The Day of Union and Love, when the kingdoms of this world become the kingdoms of our Lord and of his Christ (Rev. 11:15), when every tear is wiped away and the old order of things has passed into memory (Rev. 21:4), is just on the horizon.

THE PRAYER

Lord Jesus, I am in you and you are in me. Increase my awareness of what it means to live in union with you, and to be loved by you. I pray that I might have power from your Spirit to know that you dwell in me. I pray that I might have the power to know your love that surpasses my understanding and that I may share it with others. And I pray for your church, the body of your people called by your name, that we might come into full maturity of faith, hope, and, especially, love. In Christ Jesus, I pray, amen.

THE QUESTIONS

- What have you learned through this series?

- What Scriptures, stories, images, or ideas will stick with you and help you on your journey to know Christ Jesus and his love?

AN INVITATION TO AWAKENING

This resource comes with an invitation.

The invitation is as simple as it is comprehensive. It is not an invitation to commit your life to this or that cause or to join an organization or to purchase another book. The invitation is this: to wake up to the life you always hoped was possible and the reason you were put on planet Earth.

It begins with following Jesus Christ. In case you are unaware, Jesus was born in the first century BCE into a poor family from Nazareth, a small village located in what is modern-day Israel. While his birth was associated with extraordinary phenomena, we know little about his childhood. At approximately thirty years of age, Jesus began a public mission of preaching, teaching, and healing throughout the region known as Galilee. His mission was characterized by miraculous signs and wonders; extravagant care of the poor and marginalized; and multiple unconventional claims about his own identity and purpose. In short, he claimed to be the incarnate Son of God with the mission and power to save people from sin, deliver them from death, and bring them into the now and eternal kingdom of God—on earth as it is in heaven.

In the spring of his thirty-third year, during the Jewish Passover celebration, Jesus was arrested by the religious authorities, put on trial in the middle of the night, and at their urging, sentenced to death by a Roman governor. On the day known to history as Good Friday, Jesus was crucified on a Roman cross. He was buried in a borrowed tomb. On the following Sunday, according to multiple eyewitness accounts, he was physically raised from the dead. He appeared to hundreds of people, taught his disciples, and prepared for what was to come.

Forty days after the resurrection, Jesus ascended bodily into the heavens where, according to the Bible, he sits at the right hand of God, as the Lord of heaven and earth. Ten days after his ascension, in a gathering of 120 people on the day of Pentecost, a Jewish day of celebration, something truly extraordinary happened. A loud and powerful wind swept over the people gathered. Pillars of what appeared to be fire descended upon the followers of Jesus. The Holy Spirit, the presence and power of God, filled the people, and the church was born. After this, the followers of Jesus went forth and began to do the very things Jesus did—preaching, teaching, healing, and planting churches and making disciples all over the world. Today, more than two thousand years later, the movement has reached us. This is the Great Awakening and it has never stopped.

Yes, two thousand years hence and more than two billion followers of Jesus later, this awakening movement of Jesus Christ and his church stands stronger than ever. Billions of ordinary people the world over have discovered in Jesus Christ an awakened life they never imagined possible. They have overcome challenges, defeated addictions, endured untenable hardships and suffering with unexplainable joy, and stared death in the face with the joyful confidence of eternal life. They have healed the sick, gathered the outcasts, embraced the oppressed, loved the poor, contended for justice, labored for peace, cared for the dying and, yes, even raised the dead.

We all face many challenges and problems. They are deeply personal, yet when joined together, they create enormous and complex chaos in the world, from our hearts to our homes to our churches and our cities. All of this chaos traces to two originating problems: sin and death. Sin, far beyond mere moral failure, describes the fundamental broken condition of every human being. Sin separates us from God and others, distorts and destroys our deepest identity as the image-bearers of God, and poses a fatal problem from which we cannot save ourselves. It results in an ever-diminishing quality of life and ultimately ends in eternal death. Because Jesus lived a life of sinless perfection, he is able to save us from sin and restore us to a right relationship with God, others, and ourselves. He did this through his sacrificial death on the cross on our behalf. Because Jesus rose from the dead, he is able to deliver us from death and bring us into a quality of life both eternal and unending.

This is the gospel of Jesus Christ: pardon from the penalty of sin, freedom from the power of sin, deliverance from the grip of death, and awakening to the supernatural empowerment of the Holy Spirit to live powerfully for the good of others and the glory of God. Jesus asks only that we acknowledge our broken selves as failed sinners, trust him as our Savior, and follow him as our Lord. Following Jesus does not mean an easy life; however, it does lead to a life of power and purpose, joy in the face of suffering, and profound, even world-changing, love for God and people.

All of this is admittedly a lot to take in. Remember, this is an invitation. Will you follow Jesus? Don't let the failings of his followers deter you. Come and see for yourself.

Here's a prayer to get you started:

Our Father in heaven, it's me (say your name), I want to know you. I want to live an awakened life. I confess I am a sinner. I have failed myself, others, and you in many ways. I know you made me for a purpose and I want to fulfill that purpose with my one life. I want to follow Jesus Christ. Jesus, thank you for the gift of your life and death and resurrection and ascension on my behalf. I want to walk in relationship with you as Savior and Lord. Would you lead me into the fullness and newness of life I was made for? I am ready to follow you. Come, Holy Spirit, and fill me with the love, power, and purposes of God. I pray these things by faith in the name of Jesus, amen.

It would be our privilege to help you get started and grow deeper in this awakened life of following Jesus. For some next steps and encouragements visit seedbed .com/awaken.

THE SOWER'S CREED

Today,
I sow for a great awakening.

Today,
I stake everything on the promise of the Word of God.
I depend entirely on the power of the Holy Spirit.
I have the same mind in me that was in Christ Jesus.
Because Jesus is good news and Jesus is in me, I am good news.

Today,
I will sow the extravagance of the gospel
everywhere I go and into everyone I meet.

Today,
I will love others as Jesus has loved me.

Today,
I will remember that the tiniest seeds become the tallest trees;
that the seeds of today become the shade of tomorrow;
that the faith of right now becomes the future of
the everlasting kingdom.

Today,
I sow for a great awakening.

Printed by Libri Plureos GmbH in Hamburg,
Germany